✠

COPTIC ORTHODOX

PATRIARCHATE

See of St. Mark

Characteristics
of the
Spiritual Path

BY
H. H. POPE SHENOUDA III

Title   : Characteristics of the Spiritual Path
Author   : H. H. Pope Shenouda III.
Translated By   : Mary & Amani Bassilli.
Illustrated By   : Sister Sawsan.
Edition   : Second edition – Jan. 2000.
Press   : Dar El Tibaa El Kawmeya ,Cairo.
Legal Deposit No. : 17999/1999
I.S.B.N.   : 977 – 5319 – 99 – 4 .

H.H.Pope Shenouda III, 117th Pope and Patriarch of Alexandria and the See of St. Mark

Contents

CHAPTER THREE

CHAPTER FOUR

CHAPTER FIVE

CHAPTER SIX

CHAPTER SEVEN

CHAPTER EIGHT

CHAPTER NINE

CHAPTER TEN

CHAPTER ELEVEN

CHAPTER TWELVE

CHAPTER THIRTEEN

Introduction

In order to explain to you the spiritual path, its signs and features, and how you can walk in it, I have chosen these topics from among the numerous lectures I delivered in Saint Mark's new Cathedral at Abba Reus's Monastery during the 1960s and 70s.

First of all: What is the sound spiritual aim? And how can you remain steadfast in it? You ought to start and once you start you should continue. We shall discuss the starting point and expound how the fear of God is the beginning according to the Holy Bible (Prov.9:10). The fear of God calls you to walk in the right path even by **self-coercion** until you reach the love of spirituality and the love for God.

We shall expound **the positive work and the inner work.** Then we shall record a treatise on wisdom and discernment because wisdom should permeate and intermingle with every spiritual endeavour. Next we will talk about the general elements on which depends the uprightness of the spiritual endeavour, namely; **seriousness, commitment, meticulousness and faithfulness** in the relationship with God. This faithfulness begins by being faithful **in the few things** in our possession so that God may commend to us many.

All these are conducive to **the life of victory.** Man cannot prevail in his spiritual life unless he separates himself from all erroneous atmospheres. Thus we have written for you a treatise on 'Dividing the Light from the Darkness'.

If a person reaches the summit of the spiritual practice, he will in turn reach **the life of surrendering to God** in which he lives **the life of continuous thanksgiving.** Thence we will speak to you about these two subjects being two of the features of the spiritual path.

In addition to what we have mentioned there is a certain property of the spiritual path mentioned by the Lord of Glory Himself in the Sermon on the Mount, namely **the entrance by the narrow gate** (Matt.7:13).

Then we ask: What is the destination of the spiritual path?

The spiritual path is a journey towards perfection, the route to which is constant spiritual growth. We have also talked about this subject to you at the end of the book and added the subject of the hindrances to growth.

Do you think that we have explained to you everything related to the characteristics of the spiritual path? Undoubtedly not, because to talk about them is to talk about the whole spiritual life.

Pope Shenouda III

CHAPTER ONE

The Spiritual Goal
&
Its Constancy

The Spiritual Goal
The Reasons for Success
The Sole Goal Is God
False Aims

The Constancy of the Spiritual Goal
The Steadfast Person
Examples of Those Who Fell
Examples of Steadfastness
    Repentants
    The Martyrs
    The Divine Calling

The Spiritual Goal

My brother, you are walking along the path of life, and I wish to discuss with you a plan for your way. The first question that encounters us is: What are the reasons for the success of many?

The Reasons for Success

The answer is that the reasons for success are numerous, the first of which is that those who succeeded in life had before them strong goals which they used all their potentialities to attain.

The love of the goal and the desire to attain it gave them enthusiasm, strength, diligence and spirit. It also gave concentration and discipline to their life. Their capabilities and energies as well as their deeds were directed towards the goal without deviation.

The goal gave value to their life. They felt that there was something they lived for. Their life became delightful; a precious life with a goal. Each minute of their life became valuable. The more sublime and elevated the aim of life, the greater the value of life becomes, and the more fervently the fire in the heart burns to achieve it.

But he who lives without an aim feels that his life is monotonous and too heavy to bear. His life is meaningless and tasteless, wavering and without direction. He is restless and hesitant in all his ways. In most cases he suffers boredom and resentment, and feels that his life is worthless, wasted and trivial. He searches for means to kill time because time has neither value nor meaning to him. Many times he asks: "Why do we live? Why did God create us? What is the meaning of life? What is its aim and purpose?" Such are wretched people! They live and do not know why they live. They are dragged along by the vortex of life without them being aware, and if they become aware, they ask: "To where are we going?" However, if they find an aim for their life, all these questions vanish.

Now we would like to discuss the aims which direct people in life because it is according to the aim that the means of achieving it are defined. The aim of some is wealth or a position, title or authority, mastership or success in work. **The aim of others is pleasure, whether of the senses or of eating and drinking, or of the flesh, or of comfort.** Others' aims are to marry and have a home, or to succeed in their studies.

These cannot be called aims but we call them desires and pleasures. If they are considered aims then they are but temporary or transient or superficial aims, having no depth and limited by time. They all come under the words of the Lord to Martha: *"...you care for many things and the need is for One"* (Lk.10:41).

The Sole Goal Is God

The goal of the spiritual aspirant is God alone and none but Him. His sole aim is to endeavour to seek God, to know Him, love Him, live with Him, abide in Him, and acquire a relationship with Him. His aim is for God to dwell in his heart and for him to dwell in God's heart, so that he says to God in love: *"And there is none upon earth that I desire besides You"* (Ps.73:25). Thus by clinging to God he can do without all things. His love for God leads him to detachment and asceticism. The more he experiences and tastes the sweetness of life with God, the more he feels that everything in the world is vanity and grasping for the wind (Ecc.2:11). And as the Proverb says: *"A satisfied soul loathes the honeycomb"* (Prov.27:7), thus the soul which is satisfied with God loathes all the pleasures of the world.

False Aims

The devil, however, is not pleased with this sole aim. He goes to and fro on the earth, distributing aims. He sows and cultivates seeds of purposes, aspirations and desires so that man loses his sole spiritual aim which is abiding in God and preparing for eternal life. With all the worldly aims the devil distributes, worldly people are overwhelmed by a hell of desires which can never satisfy them, because deep inside every man is a nostalgia for infinity, and everything in the world is finite.

The first צ'ון presented by the devil is the self. To man the ego becomes an idol for him to worship. It becomes the focus and centre of all his thoughts: how he can edify it, promote it, magnify it and make it a pleasing object to everyone and the centre of their praise. He is so preoccupied with his ego that he would eliminate all else for its sake, even his relationship with God.

Thus the ego is in competition with God. At the beginning it enters the heart and stays beside God. Then it gradually takes over the whole heart and finally remains there on its own. In turning to worship the self, man continues to think every day: "What am I going to be? When am I going to be? How shall I be and how shall I advance and grow higher and greater?"

Were he to care for his self spiritually, he would sacrifice it for the sake of God and for the sake of others and live the life of love which gives itself as a ransom for others, and then he would find his self. I mean the true finding of the self, in holiness, righteousness and perfection, in God Himself. Saint Paul the Apostle, for the sake of his life with God, said: "...nor do I count my life dear to myself" (Acts 20:24). But he who gives consideration to his self entangles it with the pleasures of the world and consequently **makes the pleasures of the world his aim.** In this way he places before him the glamour of the present world and its glory, its pleasures and amusements, its dreams and aspirations. He preoccupies himself with all these so as not to think of his eternity. He remains intoxicated by worldly passions and only becomes sober at the hour of his death when he leaves the world against his will!

As for you, you shall not have this thought nor this manner, but rather **consider every aim that severs you from God and from your salvation a delusion from the devil and reject it decisively.** Reject also every means which keeps you away from your spiritual aim. Do not allow your ego to compete with God in your heart. Do not permit the world to become an aim for you. The Holy Bible says: *"...the world is passing away, and the lust of it"*, (1Jn.2:17) and *"friendship with the world is enmity with God"* (Jas.4:4).

Therefore, revise from now all your aims and all your means in the light of your concern about your eternal life and in the light of your spiritual aim which is the love of God.

Every aim against the kingdom of God is a deviation from the spiritual path. Relinquish everything that conflicts with the love of God in your heart, however great its value may be, saying to the Lord with the Apostle Saint Peter: *"...we have left all and followed You"* (Matt.19:27).

The chaste Joseph lost his freedom when he was sold as a slave, lost his reputation when he was thrown into prison, and lost his parents, brothers and country when he lived in a strange land. But God alone sufficed him. God was his aim.

He whose aim is God is not injured when he forfeits any worldly matter. God was the aim of Abraham the Patriarch. That was why it was easy for him to leave his kindred and country (Gen.12:1) and be estranged, not knowing where he was going (Heb.11:8). Rather it was easy for him to take his son and offer him as a burnt offering to the Lord.

It was easy for Saint Paul the Apostle to give up his

position, his authority and his association with leaders because none of them was his aim. He was able to say: *"I have suffered the loss of all things, and count them as rubbish, that I may gain Christ"* (Phil.3:8). Christ was his goal for Whose sake he suffered the loss of all things, without being grieved. Daniel the Prophet did not care about the royal palace nor about the high ranks nor about the king's delicacies. He did not even care about his life that he was thrown into the lions' den because he had a sole aim, before which all others grew paltry.

He whose goal is God does not make even spiritual matters his goal! Some have made prayer their goal. A person prays not because of his love for God but because he wants to be a man of prayer! He studies theology as an aim, not in order to know God and abide in Him, but in order to become a theologian, and to gain fame and a high position! Fasting also can be turned into an aim and so can every other spiritual endeavour. Man practises it either to enjoy self-satisfaction or to please other people!

However, all these spiritual practices are means and not aims. The aim is God. Prayer, fasting, knowledge, contemplation and reading are but means which lead you to your sole aim which is God, loving Him and abiding in Him. If you turn these practices into aims then you would have pursued them as ends in themselves. You may advance in them whilst you are alienated from God who said: *"These people... honour Me with their lips, but their heart is far from Me"* (Matt.15:8).

Even monasticism and dedication may turn into aims! Monasticism is but a means which leads to God. That is why its definition is the detachment from all in order to be attached to the One. If monasticism is turned into an aim, then solitude would become an aim and keeping silence would become an aim. How easily will the commandments of God be breached for their sake! The monk would detach himself from the monastery for the sake of the life of solitude. He lives as a solitary without possessing the virtues of solitude and without growing in the love of God. Thus says Saint Isaac: "There is a person who stays fifty years in a cell and does not know the way of staying in the cell".

Some people may turn correction into an aim. For the sake of correction he revolts and contends, judges and defames others, loses his love for people, his tranquillity and peace, reviles and blasphemes, and gets enraged and furious. He changes into an exploding bomb scattering sharp fragments everywhere. You look for his relationship with God in all these but you do not find it. The correction became an irreligious zeal, alienated from God and void of love.

The same happens in the ministry. Many began with the Divine service and ended with their selves. They began looking for the glory of God and ended looking for their own glory. They started to serve and their aim was God, then they put the service beside God and sometimes before Him. They concentrated on the service and it became an aim for them and they forgot God. They sought after the success of the service. Then the success of the service altered into personal success. They ended with the self. Once they reached this point, the service became a domain for showing off and for domineering. It became a mere activity and use of energy, and its means most probably became completely far from God, involving intelligence, cleverness and craftiness, and the spiritual aim which is God, was lost.

But as for you, in every spiritual deed, say with

David the Prophet: *"I have set the Lord always before me"* (Ps.16:8). Let God be your sole aim for Whose sake you serve. If the service clashes with God, leave it because how easy it is for the devil to mislead you even inside the church. Remember that the elder prodigal son was far from the love of his father even though he was serving him as he said, *"these many years"* (Lk.15:25-32)!

For this reason God asks you: "Where am I amidst your aims?"

Reply to this question with complete frankness. Is God one of your aims? Or is He the primary aim? Is He the sole aim? Or is He not an aim at all? Do you put Him at the end of your list, so that sometimes you remember Him and at others you do not? Or has God become in your opinion but a means to achieve your aims? And if He does not fulfil them for you, you get angry and enrage and may cut your relationship with Him.

Do you love God as He loved you? Is the whole of your heart for Him? Or are there side aims besides Him which you are trying to make the main aim? Are you mindful of your eternity and aware that before you reach the bosom of the saints you reach the bosom of God? Your life and your means will be dictated by your aim, so examine yourself.

The Constancy of the Spiritual Goal

The Steadfast Person

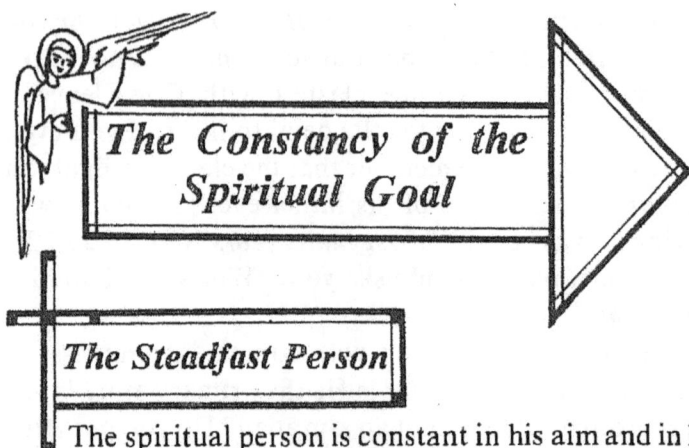

The spiritual person is constant in his aim and in his means. He has a clear, unshakeable and unchangeable aim. He concentrates all his efforts on this aim, pursuing it continually with all his efforts and desires. He does not deviate from it and all his means lead to it. He is like the arrow of the compass, always pointing in the same direction whichever way it is moved. He is a stable and steadfast person. He does not change with the changing of external circumstances nor with the vicissitude of time.

Rightly said the spiritual poet of the true man that "he advances without changing, grows in greatness without becoming haughty, and remains steady in his strides". But the weak person is hesitant. His experiences, disappointments, afflictions and circumstances in life make him change the direction of his walk and deviate from it. He may change due to temptations or fears or to a life which has opened up before him.

Thus many have started in the Spirit and then tried to be made perfect by the flesh; started with God and ....d with the world. Many people whom we knew appeared as though they had a spiritual aim but now they and their aim have no existence. They were driven, together with their spirituality, by the vortex of the world and they moved with the tide. This does not only happen in our generation but the Holy Bible presents us with amazing examples of individuals who started but did not continue, or whose aim deviated on the way and did not remain constant.

Examples of Those Who Fell

One of these personalities is Demas the assistant of Saint Paul the Apostle of whom he said: *"Demas has forsaken me, having loved this present world"* (2 Tim.4:10). What happened to Demas happened to many others of whom the Apostle Paul said in his Epistle to the Philippians: *"For many walk, of whom I have told you often, and now tell you even weeping, that they are the enemies of the cross of Christ: whose end is destruction, whose god is their belly, and whose glory is in their shame- who set their mind on earthly things"* (Phil.3:18,19).

All these were friends of the great Apostle and had a glorious past in the ministry. They had a spiritual aim with which they lived for a while but they did not abide by it because other things entered their heart besides God and with the passing of time ruled over them. Most probably they tried to compromise between God and the world. They tried to live with Sarah and Hagar in the same house or imitate the virtuous Lot who wanted to combine the love of God and the love of the green land of Sodom.

Samson began his life as a Nazirite to God and the Spirit of the Lord was moving him (Judg.13:25). Then what happened? Desires entered the heart of Samson besides God, so the Lord departed from him (Judg.16:20).

Therefore, it is not enough that your aim is the Lord. You have to remain adhering to this aim so that no other aim shall enter your heart, because you cannot bring together your vow and Delilah at the same time however wise you may think you are.

Here Solomon, the wisest of all the people on earth, gives us himself as an example. He started with a spiritual aim, there is no doubt in that. God appeared to him twice and endowed him with wisdom. Nevertheless he wanted to compromise between God and the pleasures of the world. He failed, lost his spiritual aim and fell (1Kin.11). Solomon the Sage fall? What a catastrophe! This was because the aim changed or other aims entered beside it and pulled it down. But those who adhered to their aim continued walking steadfastly towards God.

Look at the water of the Flood and what it did, and take a lesson from it. The water of the Flood covered the whole earth, even the tops of the high mountains, yet the Ark was not affected in the least by the water but rather sailed on top of it because its aim was God. No doubt God was inside the Ark, keeping and directing it. Truly the good aim gives life and energy, and ability to walk towards God. It also gives power to withstand every adverse current. The person with a constant aim is not pulled by an adverse current because his will is fixed in his aim. A small fish can withstand the tide's current and continue on its way because it has life and a will moving it, whereas a large plank of wood is pulled by the current and drawn to wherever the current takes it because it has no life and no aim.

The people of Israel left the slavery of Pharaoh, were saved from the angel of destruction and crossed the Red Sea. It was a good start, but they had no constant spiritual aim so they were destroyed in the wilderness of Sinai, even though they were fed on manna and quails and were overshadowed by the cloud of God. It could have been because their aim was themselves and how to survive, and not God and how to live with Him, so the self led them to pleasure and in turn they rebelled against God. They left the slavery of Pharaoh physically but there was another slavery inside them to which they were still bound, so they perished. The right aim was with Moses and not with the people of Israel. They could not continue to walk with him despite all the ritual worship they practised.

How easy it is for the heart which does not give itself wholly and truly to God for a genuine aim, to breach every covenant it makes with Him! It will not keep its covenants nor its promises, and will deviate towards other trivial and superficial aims which avail the person nothing.

In this way, Lot's wife left Sodom while her heart was still there. Her departure from the land of sin was not truly from the heart. It was not for the sake of God. Her hand was in the hand of the angel who directed her and her family outside the burning city, but her heart was burning with nostalgia for the things inside the city. A strange woman... she did not perish inside Sodom but after she had left it! Thus she perished and was turned into a pillar of salt. Her death became salt to the world, that is, a spiritual lesson about the danger of looking back.

The person who has a true constant aim, clinging to God, never looks back during his walk with God, lest he be reproached by Elijah who said: *"How long will you falter between two opinions? If the Lord is God, follow Him; but if Baal, then follow him"* (1 Kin. 18:21). If your aim is God, do not have two hearts and do not be hesitant.

Judas's problem was this: He sat with Christ the Lord at one and the same table and ate with Him from the same dish, and at the same time plotted against Him with the elders and leaders of the Jews. He was a disciple of the Lord with no aim. He kissed the Lord and at the same time handed Him over to His enemies. The wretched fellow lived without an aim so his life was a burden to him and to everyone else, and he perished. Nicodemus, after knowing the Lord thoroughly, could not continue to be His companion and at the same time a member of the Sanhedrin.

Ananias and Sapphira wanted to combine two aims, but they could not and perished. They wanted to keep some of their money unlawfully whilst appearing before the people as two members of the community of the children of God who put all their money at the feet of the Apostles. They profited neither the money nor the membership of the Church. They did not have the pure constant spiritual aim which does not falter between two differing ways. Their example is parallel to that of Pilate who wanted to gratify his conscience and please the Jews at the same time. When he failed, he washed his hands with water without washing his heart from within.

The rich young man wanted to combine two aims. When the Lord, the Examiner of hearts, disclosed to him his real self, he went away sorrowful. He was seeking eternal life and how to attain to it as if he had a genuine aim which he was trying to achieve, but his heart loved the present world even though he had kept the commandments from his youth (Matt.19:16-22). When the Lord revealed to him his fraility and called him to have one aim and give up all others, he went away sorrowful. Likewise will go away sorrowful whoever tries to put another aim beside God. Many say that their aim is God and at the same time try to enter by the broad gate and the broad gate in no way leads to God, because *"we must through many tribulations enter the kingdom of God"* (Acts 14:22).

Those who make God their aim ought to suffer for His sake and sacrifice themselves for His sake, knowing that their labour in the Lord is not in vain, as the Holy Bible says: *"...each one will receive his own reward according to his own labour"* (1Cor.3:8). These are the people who cling to their aim steadfastly and do not change it. They have chosen God as their target without regret or hesitation, without reconsideration and without looking back. They do not revise the matter or negotiate with the devil. The line of their life is clear and unchangeable before them. They settled it a long time before and it is no longer open to discussion, as the Apostle Saint Paul said: *"Therefore, my beloved brethren, be steadfast, immovable, always abounding in the work of the Lord, knowing that your labour is not in vain in the Lord"* (1Cor.15:58). They do not live a life of conflict between good and evil or between God and the world. Conflict signifies instability. But these people have a clear line with no hesitation or deviation to the left or right. They walk with a steadfast heart and a steadfast sight directed towards the goal. They no longer have other pleasures conflicting with their love for God. God became their sole longing desire which fills their heart to the brim leaving room for nothing else.

Examples of Steadfastness

Repentants

The stories of steadfast individuals give us an idea about the constancy of the spiritual aim. These persons left the life of sin forever and did not return to it. We never heard that Saint Augustine returned to the life of sin after his repentance, nor that Moses the Black, Saint Mary of Egypt or Pelagia returned to their former life of sin. When God became their aim, their life changed completely without any apostasy or return or a backward glance. They eradicated sin completely from their heart in utter seriousness and in wonderful sincerity to God whom they had chosen. They were like the surgeon who performs an operation to remove a cancer completely. If he gets rid of all of it but there remains even a hair's breadth, it will return, grow and become worse than it was before. That is why he who says that he has repented yet continues to fall and rise has not yet repented and his aim is still not clear before his eyes.

Repentance is not a respite from sin so that the person returns to it later on, but it is cutting every relation with sin forever and decisively, with heartfelt love for God. In defining repentance, one of the saints said that it is "exchanging passion with a longing desire", that is, the person's passion towards the world ceases and is replaced by the longing desire to live with God. This desire becomes the person's aim in life. Thus those sinners were changed not only into repentants but even into saints. They walked with such strong resolution that they applied the words of the Lord: *"And if your right eye causes you to sin, pluck it out and cast it from you; for it is more profitable for you that one of your members perish, than for your whole body to be cast into hell"* (Matt.5:29,30).

The Martyrs

Another example of the constancy of the spiritual aim is the conduct of the martyrs. Their sole aim was God and their life with Him in the blissful eternity. That is why they followed Him wholeheartedly, even to death, unheeding temptations and tortures of which none could alter their heart which abided in the Lord, as Saint Paul the Apostle said: *"Who shall separate us from the love of Christ?... For I am persuaded that neither death nor life, nor angels nor principalities nor powers, nor things present nor things to come, nor height nor depth, nor any other created thing, shall be able to separate us from the love of God which is in Christ Jesus our Lord"* (Rom.8:35-39).

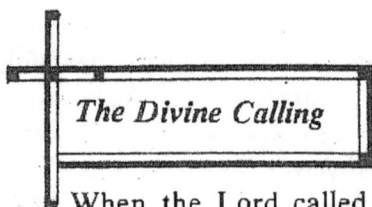

The Divine Calling

When the Lord called Abraham the Patriarch to leave his relatives, his country and his father's house for a land He would show him, Abraham did not hesitate but went out not knowing where he was going (Heb.11:8). Neither the land nor the tribe was his goal, but his goal was God for Whose sake he left everything. When the Lord ordered him to offer his only son as a sacrifice, he did not hesitate nor did he think it over nor did he suffer inner conflict. He rose up early in the morning and took his son, together with the wood, the knife and the fire. His son was not his aim but God was his aim.

Similarly, Saint Paul the Apostle said: *"But when it pleased God who separated me from my mother's womb and called me through His grace, to reveal His Son in me, that I might preach Him among the Gentiles, I did not immediately confer with flesh and blood, nor did I go up to Jerusalem to those who were apostles before me"* (Gal.1:15-17).

The Divine aim needs determination. If the devil finds in us a hesitant, indecisive, mercurial and infirm will in our relationship with God, he will know that we are like a flimsy reed which he can clutch in his grasp and crush. Let us be steadfast in our love to God. Let us not have any other aim beside Him. To Him be glory now and for ever. Amen.

CHAPTER TWO

You Start and Continue

You Start and Continue

Starting

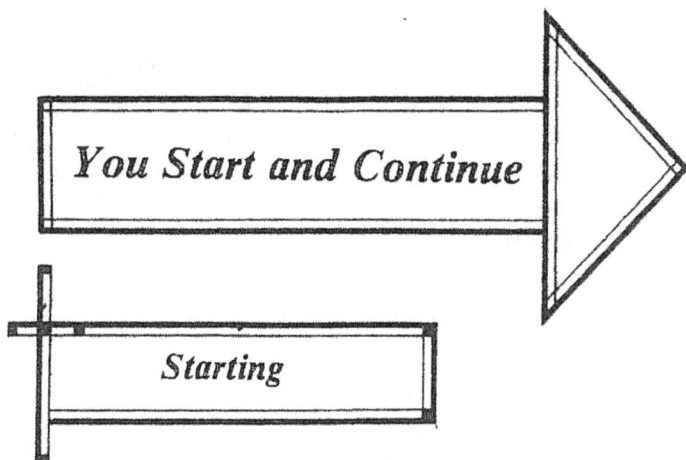

It is important that a person begins to walk in the spiritual path, to commence a relationship with God. Many have not yet started. Their life is an estrangement from God. They live an utterly secular life, engulfed in worldly material matters or in the passions of the flesh or in the various responsibilities of life. They have not yet known their way to spirituality and have not even given it a thought. They are in a labyrinth, or in a vortex or in a stupor, and consideration for eternal life has never crossed their minds.

If such people begin to give consideration to their eternal life, it will be a fundamental turning point for them.

The reasons for commencing differ from one person to another. One person may be affected by a sermon or by a book or good example, or by a spiritual person. The starting point may be a reaction to an incident or disaster or the illness or death of someone dear, or it can be one of the works of grace which awakens the conscience, directing it towards God.

A spiritual aspirant may think of commencing a serious relationship with God on a certain occasion. For example, at the beginning of a New Year or before commencing a new year of his life or on any personal occasion, he may sit alone with himself and decide to begin a new spiritual way and a more serious and active relationship with God.

Therefore, commencing may be caused by the dispensation of grace. During this period, the person may have strong zeal, spiritual fervour, decisiveness and determination, and may continue in this state for some days. The period may prolong, but then he either becomes listless, or reverts and ceases to continue what he began and his former love weakens (Rev.2:4).

Therefore, the importance is not only to begin but all the more to continue.

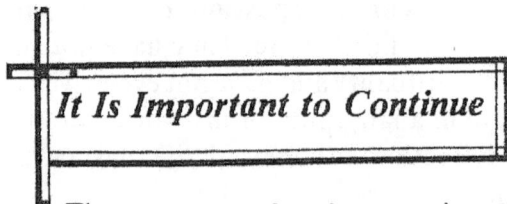

It Is Important to Continue

There are people who practise the Sacrament of Confession and partake of the Holy Eucharist, and on the day of the Holy Communion are in an excellent spiritual state and have started afresh the life of repentance with vigour and enthusiasm. Sadly, they do not continue but rather, after a few days they return to their former state before repentance.

The problem then is the problem of continuing in repentance. It is very easy for a person to live a holy life for one day. But he does not continue! A person may start an ascetic spiritual practice. For example, he says:

"I will train myself to keep silence so as to evade the errors of the tongue". He may keep silence for a day or two and not commit any error of the tongue. But he cannot continue in this practice.

It is good to have a good start but what is important is to continue. Take Saint Peter the Apostle for example. At one time he was full of zeal for the Lord, and said to Him: *"Even if all are made to stumble because of You, I will never be made to stumble"* (Matt.26:33). Beautiful words! He indeed walked with the Lord, was zealous and cut off the ear of the slave (Matt.26:51). But his zeal did not continue and he fell away and denied the Lord, and began to curse and revile, saying: *"I do not know the Man!"* (Matt.26:74).

Another example is the person who vows. When making the vow, he vows with all his emotions and is utterly ready to pay it. But he soon changes his mind. He either lingers in paying the vow or feels that it is too heavy for him to fulfil, or negotiates the possibility of altering it!

Likewise are those who make covenants with God, particularly at the beginning of spiritual zeal and ardour, or at the beginning of repentance or an ascetic practice. Yet their zeal does not continue. May I ask in this respect, those who once made covenants beyond their capabilities, some of whom vowed celibacy or monasticism and others who took a pledge on themselves not to remarry after the death of their spouse, why they did not keep their covenants? It was a zeal that did not continue. **It would have been better to raise these promises and vows to God as prayers and longing desires**

We often err and then say: "God accepted the repentance of Augustine, Moses the Black, Mary of

Egypt and Pelagia"! It is true that God accepted their repentance but the other side of this fact is that when they repented they did not return to sin but continued in their repentance and kept advancing every day a new step up the ladder of virtues. Is it so with you in your repentance?

Likewise in the ministry, many began and did not continue. Many who enjoyed distinguished names in the ministry have now no existence at all. They were driven by the preoccupations of this world and by its affairs. Their mind was engulfed by their post, family and wealth or by their education, and they abandoned the Divine service. That is why the Apostle Saint Paul says to those who minister: *"...be steadfast, immovable, always abounding in the work of the Lord, knowing that your labour is not in vain in the Lord"* (1Cor.15:58).

What we say about the ministry we also say about repentance. Many repented with ardour and tears, with covenants and vows. It was a good start for a relationship with God, but it did not last. They returned once more to their sins and most probably to a worse state, and forgot their former feelings. But the repentance of the athletic saints of repentance such as Augustine, Moses the Black, Pelagia and Mary of Egypt, was a decisive point in their lives at which they turned to the life of purity and advanced in the life of sanctity along the path of perfection.

The Outcome of Conduct

The Holy Bible tells us about the saints of God: *"...whose faith follow, considering the outcome of their conduct"* (Heb.13:7). **What matters then is the outcome of their conduct and not its beginning.** Thus in the Sinaxarium, we celebrate the days of their repose or their martyrdom and in the Diptychs, the Litany of the Departed in the Divine Liturgy, we mention "those who have been made perfect in faith".

Demas, at the beginning of his ministry, was one of the pillars of the Church. Saint Paul the Apostle mentioned him among his saintly assistants Mark, Luke and Aristarchus. But Demas did not continue in this conduct. He did not complete it and his life ended with a sorrowful sentence in which the Apostle says: *"Demas has forsaken me, having loved this present world"* (2Tim.4:10). Not only Demas, however, but many others who started the ministry with Saint Paul and were praised by him, did not continue. The Apostle finally said about them: *"For many walk, of whom I have told you often, and now tell you even weeping, that they are the enemies of the cross of Christ: whose end is destruction, whose god is their belly, and whose glory is in their shame- who set their mind on earthly things"* (Phil.3:18,19).

Therefore do not glory that you have begun, but continue so that you may attain perfection. Do not be like the person who begins to walk with God and tells everyone: "I am saved", forgetting that he ought to complete his life in faith, heeding the words of the Apostle: *"...work out your own salvation with fear and trembling"* (Phil.2:12).

Obtaining the grace of salvation through faith and baptism does not abrogate the long path before you along which you must continue walking diligently, in repentance and with good deeds, practising the Holy

Sacraments and all the means of grace, placing before you the words of Saint Paul: *"...let him who thinks he stands take heed lest he fall"*, and: *"Do not be haughty but fear"* (Rom.11:20). Therefore, be humble because the Holy Bible says about sin that she *"has cast down many wounded, and all who were slain by her were strong men"* (Prov.7:26). Saint Peter also says: *"Be sober, be vigilant; because your adversary the devil walks about like a roaring lion, seeking whom he may devour"* (1Pet.5:8).

It is good to behave fittingly but you ought to continue so that you may be saved on the Day of the Lord. And remember that the Apostle Paul upbraided the Galatians saying: *"Having begun in the Spirit, are you now being made perfect by the flesh?"* (Gal.3:3). Therefore those who begin in the Spirit should continue their spiritual path and not try to be made perfect by the flesh.

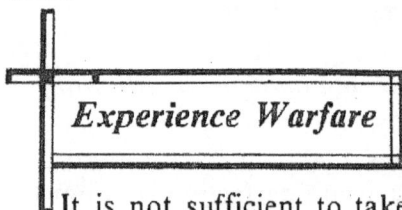

Experience Warfare

It is not sufficient to take just one step along the spiritual path, because one step does not take you to the goal. This is on the one hand. And on the other hand it does not give you any experience in the devils' combats. You must experience the devils' combats, tricks and wiles.

God may not allow the devil to wage his wars against you at the beginning of the path lest you fall into despondency. If God does allow the devil to tempt you in order to put to the test the truthfulness of your intention,

He makes the warfare very light because He has compassion on the weakness of beginners. But by God's sanction, the more a person walks in the spiritual path, the tougher the warfare becomes due to the envy of the devils. In this case God makes His grace abound towards the believer to support him in his struggle and shield him from the devils' attacks.

Thus, continuity in the spiritual path gives the person humility as well as experience. The more the person experiences the tough combats of the enemy the more he recognises his weakness before the attacks, so he humbles himself. He may fall sometimes and rise again, so he is trained on the prayers that raise him up and feels compassion for those who fall. He is also trained on patient endurance. The more he remains steadfast in the spiritual path, the more he continues walking in the path in spite of all the constraints of the enemy, remembering the words of Christ the Lord to His disciples: *"...you are those who have continued with Me in My trials"* (Lk.22:28). Yes, they continued. They were like the house built on the rock. The wind blew, and water and heavy rain poured down trying to bring it down but they could not. It was a strong house, built on the rock. It remained in its strength and steadfastness contrary to the house built on the sand which had no foundation, so could not stand and fell. **Another example is the plant which has no root and withers away** (Matt.13:6).

Having No Root

Having no root describes a person who begins the spiritual path, emerges for a while, then withdraws and disappears. He is similar to the plant which appears on the face of the earth for a while, but having no root, withers away.

What is the meaning of *"having no root"*? It is like the person who approaches the spiritual life as a result of a shock or after being affected temporarily by an incident or sermon or reading, or as a result of a major problem in which he says to God: "If You deliver me I will follow You all my life". God delivers him, so he follows Him for a little while, but having no root, he withers away. What then is the root?

The root is the life of profound faith and true love. It is the personal relationship with God, communion with Him and knowing Him, and not just outward semblances which do not spring from the heart. The person whose life is mere practices without love cannot continue.

A young lady for example hears a sermon on propriety and decent fashion and adornments. She is affected and starts to change her outward appearance but remains unchanged within. The love of God did not enter her heart to change it. True pudency, asceticism in worldliness and pursuance of eternal life were not established in her inner self. Thus she may continue for a while maintaining a decent outward appearance, but she does not continue; having no root, she withers away.

Another example is a youth who cuts his long hair due to being affected by a sermon he hears at the beginning of a New Year on ascetic practices, and not due to being convinced from within of the triviality of his outward appearance and of the need to base his manliness on sound foundations. This young man remains in his new condition for a while then leaves his hair to grow. He does not find a reason to cut it, waiting the beginning of another year or another spiritual occasion.

Thus practising religion with such persons becomes occasional, having no strong foundation and not springing from the heart out of love and faith, but is merely temporary influences and excitements which soon vanish. It is like the house built on sand, which has no foundation.

Therefore in order for a person to remain steadfast, there must be a spiritual basis sown in his heart and firmly fixed there. That is why spirituality does not begin or cease as a result of the orders of parents or superiors or spiritual guides which must be obeyed. It needs the establishment of a spiritual relationship with God, a relationship beginning within the heart based on belief in the life of the Spirit, the importance of eternity and the necessity of forming a relationship of firm love with God, and is not merely practices and outward appearances.

Spirituality begins by correcting the inner self.

The Inner Correction

For example, a person who always gets angry and enraged, raising his voice, losing his temper and mistreating others, says to himself remorsefully, "I have to train myself to abandon anger". He actually starts to train himself but does not continue because he has no root. How then can he get rid of his anger?

He has to search for the source of this sin within him and cure it. The reason for his anger might be inner pride which cannot endure an objecting word or advice or criticism. The reason might be his love of dignity and praise or a desire to enforce his own opinion no matter what it is, or to carry out his own desires. The cause of anger can be hatred towards a certain person so that he cannot stand a word from him. Whatever the reason may be, the person should cure it within himself first, then he will be able to succeed in his practices.

Therefore, we have to amend the causes and not just the symptoms. Can you cure a patient who has a high temperature with ice or aspirin? Or would you search for the cause of the rise in temperature and cure it? The cause could be tonsillitis or inflammation in a certain part of the body, or fever, and the matter needs organic treatment and not external attempts to eliminate the symptoms.

In correcting yourselves, do not merely amend the outward appearances, but amend the heart within. Rectify the actual causes from which sin springs. Then your repentance can continue and your spiritual practices can continue because they will have a firm root inside your heart. Thus the Lord said to the angel of the church of Ephesus: *"Remember therefore, from where you have fallen; repent"* (Rev.2:5).

That is why if the righteous fall they rise swiftly. David fell but he rose immediately and vigorously because the root within was sound. Peter denied Christ the Lord but he cried bitterly and repented because the root was sound, the heart within was full of love for the Lord (Jn.21:16).

The errors of those saints were venial whilst the heart within was pure. Thus we say that **their errors were sins of weakness and not sins of betrayal to the Lord.** That was the essential difference between Peter's sin and Judas's sin. Peter sinned due to weakness but Judas sinned due to betrayal. He who sins because of weakness rises swiftly as is written: *"For a righteous man may fall seven times and rise again"* (Prov.24:16).

Your love for God induces you to repent and continue in repentance. But your love for sin makes you, however much you walk in repentance, return to sin once more and continue in it. Then the cause of continuity in the former or the latter is but due to your heart and its direction. The heart which loves God is that which makes the righteous rise. And because of this heart, however much they fall, they *"shall renew their strength, they shall mount up with wings like eagles, they shall run and not be weary, they shall walk and not faint"* (Is.40:31).

Deepen your roots in the life with God. Extend them downwards before you raise trunks and branches upwards.

The inner depth supports the upward rising. A young novice in monasticism for example, pleads with his father confessor to allow him to fast long periods with hundreds of prostrations, in very strict ritual in solitude and silence. But his spiritual father says to him: "Wait, my son, until we give consideration to the inner self first. Let us lay a foundation of true love for God and of humility, meekness and gentleness in dealing with people. And on this foundation we shall build".

Therefore, care for your life and how to build it from within before you build it from without. Edify the depth before edifying the height. Edify it by rectifying the impulses before changing the outward appearances. It is not enough to abandon sin but all the more search for and eradicate its causes so as not to fall into it once more. Therefore, if you repent, you can continue in your repentance. Thus the Lord Jesus Christ said: *"Remember therefore from where you have fallen; repent"* (Rev:2:5). Uproot the thorns which surround you so that when your plant grows, it will continue to grow and will not be choked by thorns.

Delve into the depths of your inward parts, cleanse and rectify. Many begin their spiritual life by self-coercion, by suppressing their will and forcing the soul to walk in the spiritual path. We do not criticize this; it is a type of necessary spiritual striving.

But why by force? Because there is no love. You force yourself to practise virtue because the love of virtue is not in your heart. If you reach this love, self-coercion will disappear. You will practise virtue spontaneously without striving, and you will be able to walk in it without fear of falling.

This foundation of love is what we want to set in the heart because it is the safety valve. If a car's motor is functioning, the car starts by itself and does not need a manual push, but its inside- its motor- moves it. My advice to you is to care for your inward parts in order to live a constant spiritual life. If you cannot attain the love of God, place God's fear before your eyes and say as Elijah used to say, *"...the Lord of hosts lives, before Whom I stand"* (1Kin.18:15). Whenever you are attacked by a sin, say in yourself as the chaste Joseph said, *"How then can I do this great wickedness, and sin against God?"* (Gen.39:9).

Do not let your spiritual life be a mere life of occasions: If there is a spiritual revival week in the church, your spirit revives then weakens afterwards. If there is a spiritual occasion such as the beginning of a New Year or a day in which you partake of the Holy Communion or attend the Divine Liturgy on one of the Lord Feasts, your spirituality rises and then falls afterwards, with no fixed aim and no constant spiritual plan. It is not fitting that things are so. But always make your inner faith in the life with God your impetus everyday and at every hour.

Whenever you turn over a new leaf take every care to keep it clean.

CHAPTER THREE

The Fear of God & Self-coercion

The Fear of God

The Love of God and the Fear of God

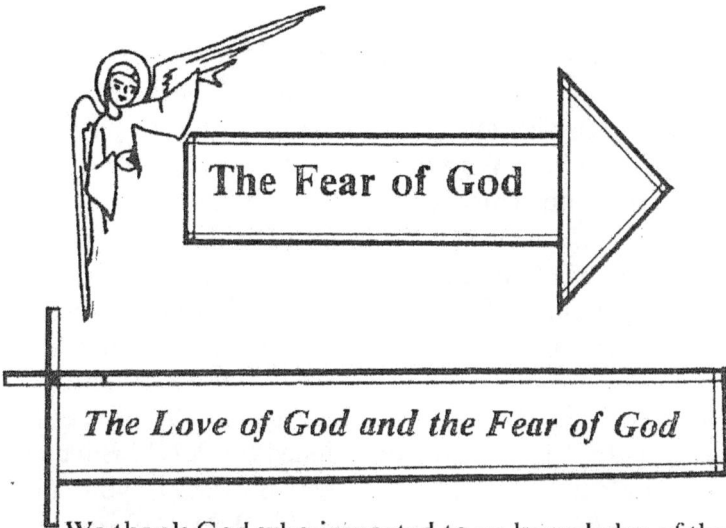

We thank God who imparted to us knowledge of the spiritual path that leads us to Him, and who laid down the characteristics of the path lest we should stray. God set regular steps for the spiritual path, each leading to the other and as a whole leading us to the sole goal, that is, God.

What then is the starting point of the spiritual path? It is the fear of God according to the words of the Divine Inspiration which are mentioned twice in the holy Scriptures: *"The fear of the Lord is the beginning of wisdom"* (Prov.9:10); (Ps.111:10).

Discourse about the fear of God may not be appealing to some people because they have been accustomed to hearing about the love of God. In fact the love of God does not at all contradict with the fear of God; it is on a higher level and surpasses it, but still keeps it. This is exactly like the student who has reached university and passed the stage of reading, writing and elementary mathematics but still employs these basics and cannot do without them.

Those who avoid the fear of God make their pretext the words of Saint John the Apostle: *"There is no fear in love; but perfect love casts out fear"* (1Jn.4:18). To reply to them we say: Who of us has reached this perfect love, the love with which you love God with all your heart, with all your soul, and with all your might (Deut.6:5); (Matt.22:37)? Have you reached the love which reigns over all your feelings to the extent that you no longer love anything in the world, confident that *"friendship with the world is enmity with God"* (Jas.4:4) and that *"If anyone loves the world, the love of the Father is not in him"* (1Jn.2:15)? Have you reached this level? Have you reached the Divine love which makes you pray continually and not lose heart (Lk.18:1), but pray with all your feelings, in deep love and with contemplation?

If you have reached this level you will not fear because your perfect love for God casts out fear. But if you have not yet reached perfect love, do not claim that you possess it and do not attribute its spiritual outcomes to your level. If you still err and fall, and are sometimes alienated from God, do not attribute perfect love to yourself. If you sometimes lose your spiritual ardour and are not profound in your prayers and contemplations, no doubt you have not yet reached perfect love, and it would be very beneficial for you to live in the fear of God.

Be confident that the fear of God is the path that leads you to love. If you fear God you will be afraid to err lest you be exposed to His retribution and wrath. You will be afraid to fall because sin severs you from God and His angels and separates you from the Kingdom and the communion of saints. That is why the fear of God prompts you to keep His commandments. When you walk in the path of God you will definitely feel the pleasure of the spiritual life, rejoice in God's commandments as one who finds great treasure (Ps.119:162) and be glad when they say to you: *"Let us go into the house of the Lord".* You will rejoice in this spiritual life and say to the Lord: *"Oh, how I love Your law! It is my meditation all the day"* (Ps.119:97). Thus you move gradually from the fear of God to the love of God, then you grow in the love of God until you reach perfect love, and fear vanishes.

God who formed our nature knows our weakness and our tendency to fall. He knows the power of our adversary the devil who walks about like a roaring lion, seeking whom he may devour (1Pet.5:8). He knows perfectly the great spiritual benefits inherent in fear. For this reason He endows us with this virtue so that we may benefit from it and gradually advance towards love in a natural and spontaneous way, and then grow in the virtue of love. What then are the spiritual benefits of the fear of God?

Benefits of the Fear of God

First of all, it is a shield against falling. The fear of God is a curb restraining us from committing sin. And if we fall, it is our impetus to repent. We say this because many jumped to the love of God without passing through His fear, and all their speech is about God the merciful, the longsuffering and loving, Who does not deal with us according to our sins nor punish us according to our iniquities (Ps.103:10). These people do

48

not understand the right meaning of love and because they are not used to the fear of God are led to indifference, recklessness and unheeding of the commandments, and consequently they fall.

So, what is love then? It is not merely feelings because the Lord says: *"He who has My commandments and keeps them, it is he who loves Me"* (Jn.14:21). And Saint John the Apostle who says that perfect love casts out fear, is himself the one who says in the same Epistle: *"Let us not love in word or in tongue, but in deed and in truth"* (1Jn.3:18). What is this practical love then? He says: *"For this is the love of God, that we keep His commandments"* (1Jn.5:3). Of course, we keep His commandments out of our love for Him but this, being a high spiritual level, should be preceded by the keeping of His commandments through fear.

People's nature is such: They are not born saints, but through the fear of God, self-coercion and vanquishing of the self, they strive until they reach love. Thus says the Apostle Saint Paul: ***"...perfecting holiness in the fear of God"*** (2Cor.7:1). So how can we perfect holiness in the fear of God? And also how can we obey the words of Saint Peter the Apostle: *"Conduct yourselves throughout the time of your sojourning here in fear"* (1Pet.1:17)?

A person should start his spiritual life with great circumspection not to fall into sin. He should fear all things that offend, temptations and the devil's combats, esteeming not his own power and resistance but putting before him the words of the Apostle: *"Do not be haughty, but fear"* (Rom.11:20).

He should also fear not to displease God, so he should put before his eyes the words of the Lord Jesus

Christ, glory be to Him: *"And do not fear those who kill the body but cannot kill the soul. But rather fear Him who is able to destroy both soul and body in hell"* (Matt.10:28), *"...yes, I say to you, fear Him!"* (Lk.12:5).

This is the fear of God's punishment. The person starts with it, and it may continue with him all the days of his life as one of the Fathers said: "I fear three things: the moment my soul leaves my body, the moment I stand before the Judgment seat of our Just God and the moment when the sentence is announced on me". Undoubtedly these three moments are fearful for anyone except those who live in perfect love for God and enjoy His holy communion at its depth, and their conscience no longer condemns them for anything. But he who fears lest any of his life be disclosed when the books are opened, should fear.

It is better for a person to fear here than to fear on the Day of Judgment because fear here induces him to repent and to reconcile with God if he wills, but fear on the Day of Judgment avails nothing. Fear here gives us the life of awesomeness and the life of tears and gives us a will to return. It is like a fence for us along the path so that we do not deviate. Thus we pray in the Thanksgiving Prayer, saying: "Grant us to complete this holy day and all the days of our life in all peace and in Your fear".

It is amazing that some people fear men and do not fear God. They are afraid to err before people so as not to be belittled in their eyes and are afraid that their sins may be disclosed to people for fear of scandal. But despite all this, they commit any sin against God with no fear as long as they commit it in secret, away from people. They misuse the loving-kindness of God. They misuse their faith in God's mercy, tender care, forgiveness and kind heart which forgave the adulteress and he who denied Him. This sadly leads them to being careless of God's prerogatives and they live their spiritual life without seriousness or commitment, as though when God does not reprimand or punish us we should not care and reach a state of indifference.

The perfect love which casts out fear is for the great saints and not for beginners in repentance nor for those who fall short in their spiritual life. Therefore, live in the fear of God. Do not jump to the love of God in a theoretical way, claiming that which you do not possess. Do not disdain the fear of God considering it a low level that does not befit you, but be utterly confident that if you are faithful in the little, that is, the fear of God, God will entrust you with much, that is, love. Therefore, walk in your spiritual life with discipline that leads you to God, taking a proper step which is conducive to another in a practical way, without longing for an outward show of spirituality which does not lead you to God.

It is true that the culmination of the spiritual life is perfect love. But you cannot start with the summit. Start with the fear of God, then you will reach the top without stumbling, particularly in this reckless generation where sin abounds and scepticism and offenses have increased, and where unbelievers and blasphemers criticize God's commandments and mock at some of them, and sometimes grumble against Him and contend with Him.

He who lives in the fear of God advances every day because he fears lest he should not reach his goal. But he who lacks the fear of God declines every day. He who fears God sees that the path of perfection stretches far before him and tries with all his might to attain it, just as the student who finds before him a long syllabus of which he has not finished a tenth and fears that he should not finish it before the examination, and his fear prompts him to increase his efforts.

We have before us a long spiritual syllabus the summary of which is two words: holiness and perfection. The Lord said to us: *"Therefore you shall be perfect, just as your Father in heaven is perfect"* (Matt.5:48). He also said: *"...be holy"* (1Pet.1:15). Who of us has reached this level? Therefore, we fear that death might overtake us before we attain our goal, and this fear prompts us to strive.

Why then do we not walk in the fear of God? The following are some of the reasons.

Causes of Fearlessness

The person who does not fear is the person who has not yet examined his self and has not known his real self and his true past, his sins and weaknesses, and does not know the spiritual level required of him and the necessary efforts and struggle he should make.

The person who does not fear God is the person who does not set the Day of Judgment before his eyes. That is why the Church reminds us of this reality every day in the prayer of the Twelfth Hour and in the Midnight Prayer so that we may wake up from our slumber in life.

The person who does not fear God is the person who is pulled by the vortex of the world, not knowing where he is going. The world enfolds him in its tumults and drowns him in its waves, drawing him into innumerable preoccupations, leaving him no time to think even of his destiny or his spiritual life. He may fall into fearlessness because the external environment which influences him has no fear of God and encourages him to lead the same life.

How can he who has not yet reached the fear of God, reach the love of God? Or rather how can he reach perfect love which casts out fear?

We do not fear because we do not set God before us, so we forget Him and His commandments, as the Psalm says about sinners: *"...they have not set God before them"* (Ps.54:3). It is also because we think of this present world and do not think at all of the world to come and the Judgment. That is why it is good that the Holy Gospel mentions that Felix was afraid when Saint Paul the Apostle talked to him about righteousness, self-control and the Judgment to come (Acts 24:25).

We reach the fear of God if we are mindful of the words of the Lord to each of the pastors of the churches of Asia: *"I know your works"* (Rev.2:2).

These are reasons hindering the fear of God but there are some practices that help us to acquire the fear of God.

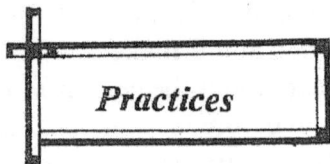

Practices

Try to fear God at least as much as you fear people. That which you are afraid to do in the presence of people, do not do before God. The thought which you fear to be known or revealed to people when you wake up from your slumber, do not dwell on before God who reads and examines all your thoughts. Know that all your thoughts will be disclosed before all creation in the Last Day, except those of which you repented and were blotted out. The hidden sins which you fear to commit before people but commit in the dark, try to be ashamed of before God who sees them.

Let God have an awesomeness which induces you to be ashamed before Him and ashamed to commit any sin before Him. Do you fear people and not God who created those people out of dust? Walk before God in pudency and know that He hears you and sees all that you do. Also give reverence to all things related to God and all that is His. Stand with reverence and solemnity in your prayer so that the fear of God enters your heart. Remember that you stand with respect before your superiors so how can you not behave the same towards God? Also revere the Holy Bible of God; do not put anything on top of it and do not read it without respect, remembering that the deacon in the church cries out, saying: "Stand in the fear of God and listen to the Holy Gospel!" If you give reverence to God's words, you will fear God Himself.

Feel shy before the angels of God who surround you, see you and hear you. Know that your dreadful sins sever you from the communion of angels who will abandon you, leaving you to your malevolent adversaries who attack you. And from this you should greatly fear. Also feel embarrassed before the souls of the saints, of your relatives and friends and even of your enemies who have departed, who see you in sin.

Walk in the fear of God so that you may reach His love. Remember the words of the Apostle: *"Love the brotherhood. Fear God"* (1Pet.2:17), and the words of the angel in the Book of Revelation: *"Fear God and give glory to Him"* (Rev. 14:7). Know that the fear of God is in the New Testament as well as in the Old Testament, and that the love of God is in the Old Testament as well as in the New Testament.

Self-coercion

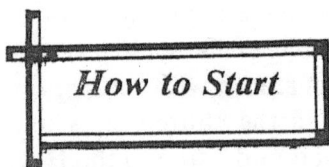

How to Start

Many spiritual counsellors differ in defining the very first virtue of the spiritual path. Some of them say that it is repentance because repentance is the turning point in the life of man, at which he leaves behind the past with all its sins and commences a relationship with God. Others say that the starting point preceding repentance is calling one's self to account and examining it. This was the starting point for Saint Augustine and the Prodigal Son.

Others say that the beginning of the path and the foundation of all virtues are humility and contrition of heart which lead to repentance and maintain its continuity. Others say that the beginning of the spiritual path is the knowledge gained through the ministry of the word. Through it principles and values are revealed to the person, influencing his concepts and feelings, and he starts a new path that leads him to giving an account of his self, repentance, contrition of heart and humility.

But some of the saints say that knowledge, giving an account of one's self and the influences are all theoretical and may be external, whilst the practical way, even within the life of repentance, is self-coercion or spiritual striving.

What Is Self-coercion?

Self-coercion means that a person forces himself to walk in the spiritual path. It is true that the spiritual life in its proper sense, is that a person loves God, loves goodness and loves the Kingdom of heaven, and walks in the life of righteousness and purity willingly from his heart, feeling that his communion with God is his complete felicity and the longing desire of his heart.

Yet do all people start at this level? No, of course not. The love of God may be the destination of the path or the culmination of the relationship with God, and not the starting point. But a person can start with the fear of God, as the Holy Bible says: *"The fear of the Lord is the beginning of wisdom"* (Prov.9:10).

A person wakes up from his slumber, and the fear of God begins to enter his heart. He fears the condemnation for his sins, fears the wrath of God, and fears that death might overtake him whilst he is not ready for it. This fear calls him to change his path.

But how does he change his path?

He changes it through self-coercion because the love

of God would not have reigned over his heart from the outset. Thus self-coercion is the practical starting point in the spiritual life. The beginner in the spiritual path is not trained on prayer. He is not used to stand long before God and has no spiritual feelings to help him pray with love, tenderness of heart, solemnity and contemplation. Yet he forces himself to pray, and if he is tempted to conclude his prayer he forces himself to continue. He feels at night that he is weighed down by slumber and physically exhausted, having neither the energy to stand for prayer nor the desire to pray. Yet he forces himself, putting before his eyes the words of Saint Isaac: "Force yourself on the night prayer, enhancing it with psalms." In this way the person forces himself to pray, to stand or kneel or make prostrations. He forces himself to lift up his hands, to concentrate his senses in prayer and to control his scattered intellect, restraining it from straying and wandering.

Self-coercion and Growth

One of the Fathers said: "If you wait until you reach pure prayer and then start to pray, you will never pray". This is because the pure prayer is not the starting point but it is the culmination of the spiritual endeavour. As for you, force yourself to pray even if your prayer is weighed down by slumber, or with scattered intellect or void of contemplation. God may look at your exertion and striving, your patient endurance and perseverance, and irradiate you with His grace or uplift you a step towards prayer.

We say the same about every other virtue. You may start to fast without having the love for fasting or the intense desire for hunger, but you force yourself to fast. You may not have a longing desire to read the Holy Bible or contemplate its words, but you force yourself to read it. Similarly, you force yourself to repentance, confession and attending spiritual gatherings. You force yourself to forgiveness, paying the tithes, consecrating the Day of the Lord, restraining the tongue and controlling the senses. The same applies to keeping silence and controlling the intellect. If you cannot force yourself to resist the errors of the tongue, pray, saying: *"Set a guard, O Lord, over my mouth; keep watch over the door of my lips"* (Ps.141.3).

Self-coercion Is a Transitional Virtue

Someone may ask: Does God accept the virtue which is void of love and practised forcibly? I say, first of all, it is not void of love. Without love you cannot practise it. But it is a preliminary love resisted by the habits of the old man, resisted by the attachment to the flesh and material things, and resisted by the devil's attacks and various other hindrances. And God accepts this self-coercion as a type of spiritual striving and as an attempt to vanquish the self. Solomon the Sage said: *"...he who rules his spirit* (is better) *than he who takes a city"* (Prov.16:32). God knows that the spiritual endeavour is not easy for beginners, and He knows what the beginner encounters due to the envy of the devils and their assaults.

It is likely that for the need of forcing one's self to walk in the spiritual path, that the Lord said: *"Enter by the narrow gate; for wide is the gate and broad is the way that leads to destruction, and there are many who go in by it. Because narrow is the gate and difficult is the way which leads to life, and there are few who find it"* (Matt.7:13,14). Yet the gate does not remain narrow all the way through, but only at the beginning. The more a person practises the spiritual act, the more he finds pleasure in it and the more he finds new life in it attracting him. So he completes it and pursues it with an ardent heart. Thus he may start to pray by forcing himself, but once he finds spiritual enjoyment in prayer he practises it diligently and with love.

The devil, however, ridicules this self-coercion, attempting to use it as a means to stop the spiritual endeavour. He says to you: "Is it decent to speak to God thus by forcing yourself to pray? Where is the love of which David the Prophet said: *'I will lift up my hands in Your name. My soul shall be satisfied as with marrow and fatness'?* " (Ps.63:4,5). Then he calls you to discontinue your prayer for the sake of respecting the ideality of the pure prayer which is full of love and awe! And it is impossible that you start with perfection.

It is important for the devil to stop you from praying. In the same way he attempts to stop every spiritual endeavour by mocking at the state of self-coercion which might have been caused by him. But God sees the meaningless sounds articulated by the little infant as the beginning of his way towards perfection. He sees the toddling of the baby as the primary steps of walking regularly and speedily. The world champions in jumping, running and swimming began their childhood with awkward movements, then gradually they reached perfection. That is why we do not disdain self-coercion nor does God despise it, but He rather encourages it so that a person can grow and walk towards the Divine love.

What is important is that self-coercion should not remain but should be a mere step conducive to a better one. An example of self-coercion which gradually leads to love is almsgiving. The Holy Bible says that *"God loves a cheerful giver"* (2Cor.9:7). Will you refrain from giving until you reach the standard of a cheerful giver, or the standard of *"he who gives with liberality"* (Rom.12:8)? Why should the poor or the needy who are in need of your donation bear the brunt of your not having reached this standard?

The right attitude is that you give even if by forcing yourself. Force yourself to pay the tithes for the sake of the poor who need it. Then advance to force yourself to pay the firstfruits, the vows and all what is due God of your possessions. From there you advance to expend all that you have for others and you no longer force yourself in giving. You may ask, "How?" Whenever you perceive the happiness of people and that their problems are solved by what you give, their happiness will be conveyed from them to you making you rejoice in giving, so you give cheerfully and generously. You will find that self-coercion has left you, because it is not a constant but a transitional virtue. If God gives reward for the love in every virtue, He also gives reward for self-coercion, not forgetting your labour in overcoming the obstacles which encounter you from without and from within yourself.

Through self-coercion you surrender your self, your body and your will. The animal on whose neck they lay a yoke to draw a cart, a plough, a dirt scraper or a threshing machine, may at the beginning, refuse, resist and flee but by intimidation he easily bends his neck under the yoke to carry out his duty quietly and contentedly. His resisting was at a primary stage. Grumbling, escaping and refusing were a stage which ended in satisfaction. How much more deserving is he who forces himself to carry out the spiritual endeavour. Training oneself on self-coercion includes what we call the spiritual practices.

The spiritually mature person does good of his own accord but the beginner needs to practise. He may fail a little in his practices at the beginning but through self-coercion, persistence and spiritual striving, he changes the practice into a permanent quality, deeply rooted in him. Saint Paul the Apostle says: *"Everywhere and in all things I have learned both to be full and to be hungry, both to abound and to suffer need"* (Phil.4:12). The more difficult the practice is, the greater the reward will be. Self-coercion entails strengthening one's will and directing it towards goodness.

Benefits of Self-coercion

Self-coercion is greatly beneficial in overcoming the bad habits which have dwelt in the person for a long time, subduing, humiliating and enslaving him. It is not easy for the person to abandon them willingly but he needs to force himself, to compel his inner self to obey him whilst leading it in a reverse direction to which it was used. Self-coercion is undoubtedly a rebellion against pampering the soul, or it is a war waged against the ego. We all know that if a person gives way to his desires and passions, enjoying slothfulness and indolence, he will no doubt lose his soul. But through self-coercion he does not leave his inner self to its passions, but he commands and it obeys, he directs it and it submits even by compelling it against its wishes until it attains the love of goodness and the love of God.

We sometimes use coercion in bringing up our children, because if we spoil them and leave them to their wishes the inevitable result is their loss and perdition. We use this discipline for their own good when the way of love, kindness, convincing and coaxing, fails.

When Jonah the Prophet did not force himself to obey God, God forced him. When he escaped from God, God ordered a great fish to swallow him and bring him back to God's obedience. Many people did not wake up quickly and return to God by love. They returned to Him by force through various trials and afflictions.

It is better for a person to force himself than to be forced by events and trials. The difference between the saints and ordinary people is that the saints forced themselves to practice virtue from the beginning until they got used to it and loved it. They had flesh like ours which suffered hunger and thirst, and they forced themselves to fast. They had bodies that became weary and exhausted but they forced themselves to vigils as did Abba Pishoi who used to tie his hair to a rope on the ceiling to pull it up whenever his head bent with slumber. And as did David the Prophet who made a covenant with himself, saying: *"Surely I will not go into the chamber of my house, or go up to the comfort of my bed; I will not give sleep to my eyes or slumber to my eyelids, until I find a place for the Lord"* (Ps.132:3-5).

Advice and Practices

Do not respond to the love of ease nor to the call of desire. Do not spoil yourselves but know that self-coercion will continue with you until you find pleasure in the life of virtue and then it will leave you spontaneously and the life of love will start.

Put before you an important spiritual rule, that is, the biggest war we fight in our spiritual life is the war against ourselves. If we prevail from within through self-coercion we will overcome every other war from without.

Do not carry out every thought that enters your mind, nor any desire that knocks at your heart. If you cannot refrain, postpone the matter for a while, then force yourself to keep postponing. During postponing the grace of God may visit you and comfort you. Know that self-coercion comes under the Lord's commandment of carrying the cross (Matt.16:24), because *"those who are Christ's have crucified the flesh with its passions and desires"* (Gal.5:24).

Try to rebel against your ego and against your passions. Lay down for yourself a fixed spiritual discipline and force yourself to put it into practice. Do not permit yourself some exceptions which signify slackness, indifference and lack of seriousness in the spiritual endeavour.

The principle of self-coercion appears in the words of the Lord: *"And if your right eye causes you to sin, pluck it out and cast it from you; ..And if your right hand*

causes you to sin, cut it off and cast it from you"
(Matt.5:29,30). Thus you force yourself, not yielding to
your eyes when they desire to look, but you restrict them
and you also restrain your hands.

Likewise, in preventing the tongue from speaking we
see that Saint James the Apostle uses terms signifying
self-coercion such as bridle, tame, and control. For the
sake of self-coercion the nations laid down laws and
punishments and God also gave commandments as well
as punishments.

Spiritually, a person is to force himself to abandon
evil and do good before he is forced to do so by law,
commandments and punishments. Good is requested to
spring from within the person's heart, by his own will, by
forcing himself to abandon errors without him being
compelled to do so with no reward.

Let your conscience force you and not the law. Rise
above the standard of the law so as to reach the love of
goodness. Force yourself to do good before you force
others. If you err, punish your inner self instead of
receiving punishment from without.

CHAPTER FOUR

The Spiritual Conduct and Uprightness

The Spiritual Conduct

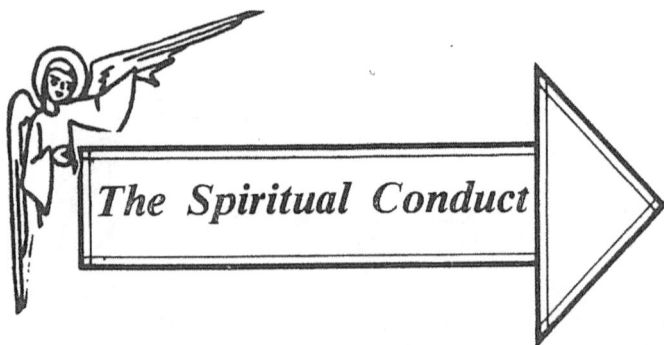

The spiritual person walks according to the Spirit. He walks as the Spirit directs and leads him, and not according to the flesh and its desires and materiality. He who walks according to the Spirit is acceptable to God, whereas he who walks according to the flesh falls under condemnation. This is why Saint Paul the Apostle said: *"There is therefore now no condemnation to those who are in Christ Jesus, who do not walk according to the flesh, but according to the Spirit"* (Rom.8:1).

Naturally, the spiritual aspirant should care for his spirit, for her nourishment, fitness and growth. In order to keep her strong and growing he should give her the nourishing necessities of all the means of grace, such as prayer, fasting, spiritual readings, contemplations, prostrations, spiritual gatherings, spiritual retreats and spiritual counselling. He should also enable his spirit to grow in the life of virtue through love that binds him with God and through the life of repentance which preserves the purity of his spirit.

Notwithstanding, the vast majority of people are more concerned about their bodies than their spirits. They give all their attention to the body and to all things related to it such as food and drink, clothing and housing, recreation and adornment. They care for the desires of the flesh, fulfilling its lusts and pleasures in a way that absorbs all their intellect and emotion, even if it conflicts with the purity of their spirit. These persons forget the words of the Apostle: *"For to be carnally minded is death, but to be spiritually minded is life and peace. Because the carnal mind is enmity against God...So then, those who are in the flesh cannot please God"* (Rom.8:6-8).

This is why such people are called carnal, and carnal people cannot inherit the kingdom of God because it is a spiritual Kingdom where abide only those who walk according to the Spirit. When the Apostle talked about the love of the world, that it is enmity with God, he said: *"For all that is in the world - the lust of the flesh, the lust of the eyes, and the pride of life"* (1Jn.2:16), he placed the lust of the flesh the first of worldliness. Here we ask a pressing question:

Is the Body a Sin?

No, the body is not a sin nor an evil otherwise God would not have created it. It suffices that God took a body, and moreover, the Apostle says to us: *"Or do you not know that your body is the temple of the Holy Spirit who is in you?"* and: *"Do you not know that your bodies are members of Christ?"* (1Cor.6:19,15). If this is the case of the body then it is not evil. And God will raise this same body on the Last Day as a spiritual and an illumined body (1Cor.15). Moreover, if the body were a sin we would not venerate the bodies of the saints.

The body is holy because it was immersed into the water of baptism and was consecrated and took a new nature. It was anointed with the holy Chrism of Myroon and became a temple for the Lord (1Cor.3:16). This is the right view with which we respect the body and look upon it with dignity, whether our own body or other people's, remembering the words of the Apostle: *"If anyone defiles the temple of God, God will destroy him"* (1Cor.3:17), *"...therefore, glorify God in your body and in your spirit which are God's"* (1Cor.6:20).

Then we can glorify God in and with our body. Does the body not join the spirit in worshipping God? The spirit prays and the body stands or kneels or makes prostrations or lifts up pure hands and pure eyes. The body fasts, the body blesses God in making prostrations, the body toils in the service and in helping others. If we respect the body in this way we will never humiliate or defile it whether our body or the body of others.

We look on the body as a small church, holy and consecrated with Myroon, in which the Spirit of God dwells. It is assumed that out of this small church come praises, prayers, hymns, psalmody and spiritual songs (Eph.5:19) which are raised up to God as incense, according to the Psalmist's words: *"Let my prayer be set before You as incense, the lifting up of my hands as the evening sacrifice"* (Ps.141:2).

This is the spiritual view of the body. Therefore, the body is not a sin if we use it in a spiritual way and understand it in a spiritual way. It is something holy, as the bodies of Adam and Eve before sin, the bodies of the righteous in the general resurrection, and as every body of the living who bless God. How then can we keep the body holy?

The Subjection of the Body to the Spirit

The body will be holy if it submits to the direction of the spirit and not vice versa. If the former happens the person will walk in a spiritual way, conforming to the words of the Apostle: *"I beseech you therefore, brethren, by the mercies of God, that you present your bodies a living sacrifice, holy, acceptable to God, which is your reasonable service. And do not be conformed to this world"* (Rom.12:1,2). Therefore, the body can be a holy and living sacrifice.

If the body resists and does not submit to the spirit, then the words of the Holy Bible: **"For the flesh lusts against the Spirit, and the Spirit against the flesh; and these are contrary to one another"** (Gal.5:17), will apply to the person.

The Apostle does not say this about all bodies but about the erring bodies which resist the work of the Spirit and which lust against the Spirit, causing man to suffer inner conflict between his body and his spirit. But the saints were not like this; their bodies joined with their spirits in the spiritual work, expending themselves. That is why God rewards the body and grants it to rejoice with the spirit in the eternal bliss in His kingdom. Thus in the prelude to walking in the Spirit, man's spirit subjugates the body, preventing it from walking in the materialistic way but rather inducing it to walk in the spiritual path. Thus said Saint Paul the Apostle: *"But I discipline my body and bring it into subjection, lest, when I have preached to others, I myself should become disqualified"*

(1Cor.9:27). In like manner behaved all the Fathers in the wilderness and cells until their bodies became completely pliable to their spirits and joined in the spiritual endeavour of fasting, vigil and prostrations. They did not give their bodies their lustful desires.

Therefore, the body in itself is not a sin but the lust of the flesh is. Our forefathers Adam and Eve fell into the lust of the flesh when they looked at the tree of knowledge of good and evil and saw that it was good for food, pleasant to the eyes and a tree desirable to make one wise (Gen.3:6). Thence started the deviation towards desiring what is material and what is carnal. Here the Holy Bible warns: *"For if you live according to the flesh you will die; but if by the Spirit you put to death the deeds of the body, you will live"* (Rom.8:13).

This is why the saints entered into deeds of mortification in order to put to death the passions of the body. Thus we entreat the Lord Jesus Christ in the Ninth Hour Prayer, saying, "Mortify our carnal senses". If our carnal senses die, that is, they no longer activate to insinuate into the heart passions and desires, then the spiritual senses shall live and move by the love of God. Thus says the Holy Bible: *"But you are not in the flesh but in the Spirit, if indeed the Spirit of God dwells in you"* (Rom.8:9). If a person lives in the Spirit and by the Spirit and the body submits, then he will enjoy the life of victory over matter and over the world. Thence the person becomes one being, not two conflicting ones. Consequently there will be no inner conflict between the body and the spirit. The body will desire what the spirit desires and both will co-operate in every righteous deed. **Then the body will not sin.**

The Body and Sin

The body which sins is the body which rebels against the spirit, or it is the body which controls the spirit and subjects her to its pleasures. The spirit is consequently defiled with the body and loses her Divine image, falling with the body under condemnation in that fearful Day.

The body which errs is in effect defiling one of God's temples because the body is God's temple. If it sins it is as though someone is destroying a holy church in which God dwells. **The body does not only rebel against its own spirit but also against the Spirit of God who dwells in it.**

If we say that the person whose spirit prevails, leading the body to the life of holiness becomes like the angels of God in heaven, it follows that the person whose body directs the spirit and rebels against the spirit is degraded to the level of the animals.

The body which lives in its lusts is considered dead even though it is throbbing with life, as the Apostle said: *"...the body is dead because of sin"* (Rom.8:10). That is why the Lord said to the pastor of the church of Sardis: *"I know your works, that you have a name that you are alive, but you are dead"* (Rev.3:1). And the Apostle said about the dissipated widow that *"she who lives in pleasure is dead while she is alive"* (1Tim.5:6), because the true life is in God and he who is separated from God by sin is considered dead even though he is alive. The father said about the prodigal son: *"...for this my son was dead"* (Lk.15:24). And he who repents returns to life as was said about the prodigal son when he repented: *"...for* *this my son was dead and now is alive again"* (Lk.15:24). That is why a person ought to care for his spirit. In this way he would be caring about his eternity.

Caring for the Spirit

The Apostle says: *"To be spiritually minded is life and peace"* (Rom.8:6). The person puts before him that he has one spirit, and that if he directs her to the way of salvation, he profits everything, but if he loses this spirit, he loses everything. And as the Lord Jesus Christ said: *"For what is a man profited if he gains the whole world, and loses his own soul"* (Matt.16:26).

He who walks in the spiritual path concerns himself wholeheartedly with purifying his spirit and connecting her with God, aspiring that she inherits the kingdom of God in the blissful eternity. **He walks in the Spirit, grows in the Spirit and becomes a spiritual person.** He returns to the image of God and preserves himself continually in the image of God. The spirit is the breath which God breathed in man and he became a living spirit whereas the body is the earthly element because it was created out of the dust of the earth. Through spiritual conduct man becomes similar to the angels and has friendship and communion with God, with His angels and with the whole spiritual world. Rather, he himself becomes an angel of God. His behaviour becomes spiritual, his words become spiritual, his relations become spiritual and the Spirit governs his whole life.

Therefore, my brother, consider how you walk. Do you walk in the Spirit or in the flesh? The Holy Bible says: *"Walk in the Spirit, and you shall not fulfil the lust of the flesh"* (Gal.5:16), and furthermore: *"...be filled with the Spirit"* (Eph.5:18). Here the spiritual growth is manifest, from walking in the Spirit to the Spirit-filled life.

The Relation of Your Spirit to the Spirit of God

The spiritual person submits his body to his spirit and submits his spirit to the Spirit of God. This becomes proof of his sonship to God. To this effect the Holy Bible says: *"For as many as are led by the Spirit of God, these are sons of God"* (Rom:8:14). If the Spirit of God directs a person, he does not sin and *"the wicked one does not touch him"* (1Jn:3:9), (1Jn.5:18). And indeed this is how the children of God are marked out from others.

The matter is not only limited to the negative side of abandoning sin but from the positive side the fruit of the Spirit is manifest. Concerning this the Apostle said: *"But the fruit of the Spirit is love, joy, peace, longsuffering, kindness, goodness, faithfulness, gentleness, self-control"* (Gal.5:22,23). This he said about those who walk in the Spirit, *"those who are Christ's have crucified the flesh with its passions and desires"* and added at once: *"If we live in the Spirit, let us also walk in the Spirit"* (v.25).

How can we say that we are children of God if we are not led by the Spirit of God? And how can we say that we live in the Spirit if the fruit of the Spirit is not apparent in our life?

The person who is led by the Spirit of God does not quench the Spirit nor grieve the Spirit of God within him and does not resist the Spirit of God but he completely resigns to the work of the Spirit within him. He is a pliable instrument to the Holy Spirit, by whom God performs His holy will. He does not betray God by opening the doors of his heart or of his mind to sin which resists the work of the Spirit but on the contrary, he co-works with the Spirit of God. Thus he enters into fellowship with the Holy Spirit (2Cor.13:14) and becomes a partaker of the Divine nature (2Pet.1:4) working for his salvation and for the salvation of others.

Therefore, walking in the Spirit is walking in your spirit and in the Spirit of God. Then your spirit will be beautified with virtues, ready to meet God *"as a bride adorned for her husband"* (Rev.21:2). Your spirit will be adorned with the virtues of love and humility, faith and labour for the sake of God, and you will be adorned with the *"ornament of a gentle and quiet spirit, which is very precious in the sight of God"* (1Pet.3:4), as Saint Peter the Apostle said.

Therefore, concern yourself with the beauty of your spirit so that when you take off your body, your spirit will be acceptable in heaven, having the pleasing aroma of Christ. And your spirit will have an awesomeness even in this world before the devils: *"A thousand may fall at your side, and ten thousand at your right hand; but it shall not come near you"* (Ps.91:7). Do you want, then, to test yourself and see whether or not you walk in the Spirit? Take this question: **Do you fear the devils or do they fear you because the Spirit of God dwells in you?**

Walk, my brother, in the Spirit and you will reach this level, and in every deed you do, trust that God works it with you through His Holy Spirit. Preserve the indwelling of the Holy Spirit within you.

Uprightness

The Meaning of Uprightness

The spiritual person is an upright person. He is upright in his thoughts, in his conscience, and in his conduct before God and men. What is the meaning of this uprightness and what are its features? How can it be attained? How is it tested? And how can we distinguish it?

An upright person is a just person. He does not behave wrongly either consciously or unconsciously. He does not combine truthfulness with falsehood. He walks in a straight path from which he does not stary, as the Divine Inspiration says: *"Do not turn to the right or to the left"* (Prov.4:27), that is, do not swerve either to the right or to the left.

Uprightness Versus Extremity

Exaggeration in the spiritual path is not acceptable, whether it be exaggeration in words or in description or in behaviour, because exaggeration in words and description are kinds of telling lies. Neither of them gives the real picture. Exaggeration in behaviour is not upright because it is a type of extremity and may turn into pharisaism. To this effect, referring to his life before the Faith, Saint Paul the Apostle said: *"...according to the strictest sect of our religion I lived a Pharisee"* (Acts 26:5).

Those who are strict with themselves become accustomed to rigidity and they constrain others. Then their judgment becomes unjust, cruel and perverted. The Lord Jesus Christ upbraided the scribes and pharisees because they bound heavy burdens, hard to bear, and laid them on men's shoulders (Matt.23:4), thus falling into the sin of obduracy and of censuring others. In this attitude, they gave people an unobtainable picture of the kingdom of God, causing them to fall into despondency for not being able to attain to it. Thus they closed the Kingdom of heaven before people. They neither got in themselves nor allowed those who were entering to go in (Matt.23:13).

Extremity lacks steadfastness. The person may be extreme in the way he fasts and may continue in this way for some time. He may think that he has been raised to a high spiritual level but suddenly he is unable to continue. He may revert to a much lower level than those who walk in the way slowly, gradually and gently. The same is said about prostrations and all other works of asceticism and mysticism. In keeping silence to try to avoid the sins of the tongue, a person may go to extremes, imposing on himself severe practices which he cannot keep for long. Moreover, this silence in its extremity might cause him to fall into various errors, worsening his relationships with people, and his behaviour would be remote from uprightness.

The behaviour which fluctuates up and down without stability is not an upright behaviour and does not conform to the advice of the holy Fathers. The spiritual Fathers used to counsel their disciples to avoid extremity because on the one hand it does not agree with the truth and on the other it lacks continuity and may cause the person to change to the opposite extreme.

This vacillation in the spiritual life does not comply with the uprightness of the sound spiritual walk. For this reason the Fathers used to recommend gradualness; from an easy feasible start, free from self-conceit and haughtiness, growing by degrees until the goal is attained. They used to say: "Little with continuity is better than much with intermission". Any spiritual endeavour which the person begins and continues in for a long time until it settles and becomes stable in him then grows in a quiet, gradual and steadfast manner is far better than a high spiritual leap which does not continue for long followed by a relapse. Leaps in the spiritual life are perilous and unstable and in most cases reaped by the devil of vainglory.

Uprightness Versus Falsehood

If extremity is wrong even in what the person may think to be right what then shall we say about falsehood involving extremity? The person might walk in falsehood through ignorance. Nevertheless, his behaviour is condemned as being void of uprightness. His way is not straight because it is against truth and against righteousness whether or not he is aware of it. How deep are the words of the Holy Bible: *"There is a way that seems right to a man, but its end is the way of death"* (Prov.16:25;14:12). It is not a straight way and its end is death no matter how different it seems to the person.

Pride may visualize to the person that all his behaviour is straight whereas the truth could be the complete opposite. In this respect the Holy Bible says: *"The way of a fool is right in his own eyes"* (Prov.12:15). Uprightness needs a humble heart which perceives its errors and rectifies its ways. But the haughty person continues in his wrong behaviour because he rejects acknowledging the errors of his way. Thus we observe the strong relation between uprightness and humility. The haughty person does not know his reality thoroughly nor does he recognize his fall or acknowledge it. That is why the Holy Bible describes him as a fool and says that the way of a fool is right in his own eyes.

A person may walk in falsehood due to an illness and subsequently loses the uprightness of his conduct. For example, a person who is psychologically ill may think that people are against him, persecuting him. So he hates some of them, resists others, reviles some, complains of all and is complicated, thinking that dangers are darting at him from everywhere when there are no dangers at all. Such a person loses the uprightness of his behaviour as a result of his psychological disorder. Nevertheless the behaviour of such a person is considered lacking uprightness. Falsehood is falsehood, whether or not a person is condemned for committing it. We do not say that the mentally ill person is not upright but we say this about his behaviour.

There is a person who tries to combine truthfulness with falsehood and this is not upright because the falsehood which he sometimes falls into distorts the uprightness of his way and can never comply with the characteristics of the spiritual path. But if he confesses his errors and straightens his way, we consider that it was a sin of which he repented. The danger is when a person considers the falsehood in which he walks a type of uprightness. He clothes it with robes of virtue and considers himself right in all his errors, but as he does not call them errors, consequently they remain with him. He does not repent of them and does not change his principles nor his manner of assessing matters. With such a person, the lack of intellectual and conscientious uprightness becomes the cause of his habitual perverted behaviour.

How dangerous is a morally dishonest conscience in which the person loses the balance of his criteria and values, and his judgment on matters lacks integrity! He commits the sin with a complacent conscience when in fact it is a sick or perverted conscience. Such persons need awareness and spiritual instruction to correct their spiritual criteria. For those who accept being instructed, there is hope for their return to uprightness of mind, conscience and behaviour.

Uprightness Versus Hypocrisy

Some persons try to combine truthfulness and falsehood through hypocrisy. The outward appearance of such people is straight whilst from within they are the contrary. They appear to people as righteous whilst they are sinners. They are like whitewashed tombs which indeed appear beautiful outwardly, but inside are full of dead men's bones and all uncleanness. Through hypocrisy they combine two types of perversion: their erring inside is not straight, and their outward appearance of uprightness is an act of dishonesty. Thus they fall into dual sin. Because if the person who does good in order to show people his righteousness falls into the sin of hypocrisy how much more hypocritical will be the perverted person who appears to people as though he is upright and virtuous! This is a double hypocrisy. Judas was of this kind. He kissed Christ the Lord as a friend whilst he was handing Him over to His enemies with a kiss. He sat next to Him, ate with Him, dipped his morsel in the same dish whilst he had received the price of his conspiracy against Him. Judas's betrayal was one thing but his continuity in following Christ and His disciples, eating with Him and kissing Him was another type of perversion which manifested itself in hypocrisy and pretended love.

Of this kind was Delilah with Samson, the same

blend of treason and hypocrisy. She showed him love and intimacy whilst she handed him over to his enemies. With the same hypocrisy and on a much higher level behaves the devil. While he pretended that he was offering Adam and Eve the way of glory, he was acting towards their destruction. And with us he acts in the same manner. The hypocrite person often has two faces and two tongues. Thus he is not upright in his behaviour. Another example is Balaam who tried to combine the money of Balak the son of Zippor with the construction of seven altars for the Lord (Num.22,23). He said: *"How shall I curse whom God has not cursed? Must I not take heed to speak what the Lord has put in my mouth?"* (Num.23:8,12). And at the same time he presented Balak with the advice with which he would destroy the people (Rev.2:14). Balaam thought that it was enough that his tongue did not utter a curse to the people whilst his heart was seeking their destruction. But the upright person's heart and tongue are together in one integral direction.

The Lord Jesus Christ rejected the tongue and the heart being in two opposite directions and He repeated the phrase which was said about the people in the Old Testament: *"These people draw near to Me with their mouth, and honour Me with their lips, but their heart is far from Me"* (Matt.15:8); (Is.29:13). When the upright person says a word of love or praise with his lips, his heart bears the same feeling. There is no contradiction between the heart and the tongue because contradiction is an indication of lack of uprightness.

In this contradiction fall those who use flattering words, untrue praise and hypocritical phrases. Among those who fell into this error were the false prophets who said to King Ahab that he would prevail (1 Kin.22:13-22).

Policies and purposes do not lead an upright person nor do they alter his conscience and his tongue. He does not walk in hypocrisy for the sake of achieving a purpose or gaining fame or joining a certain current. But he is the same inwardly and outwardly. He is not two persons, but one. He does not behave contrary to his conscience to say what pleases people, and does not say except what he believes in his heart to be true.

Hypocrisy is contrary to uprightness because it is an attempt to combine two opposing directions in a deceiving manner.

Uprightness Versus Deception

Jacob was not upright when he deceived his father Isaac and told him that he was his firstborn son Esau (Gen.27:19). Neither was he upright when he put the skins of the kids of the goats on his hands and on the smooth part of his neck. His mother Rebekah was not upright when she advised him of all this, adding that may his curse fall on her (Gen.27:13).

Joseph's brothers were not upright when they deceived their father Jacob by dipping Joseph's many-coloured tunic into the blood of a kid of a goat so that their father might think that he was devoured by a wild beast (Gen.37:31-33).

The upright person is open and explicit. He does not lie or deceive, neither does he attain his purpose or solve his problems through deceit. In his sight deception is not an upright method and he despises himself if deceit leads him to his purpose.

Deceit is against truth. The upright person is truthful. He does not allow himself to be unfair to others. If he has an aim he wishes to attain, he will obtain it through an upright way because he believes not only in the uprightness of the purpose and the aim, but also in the uprightness of the means. He rejects artfulness.

Uprightness Versus Artfulness

If a crooked person does not reach his aim through upright means, he employs trickery. And if he still does not succeed, he employs artfulness. This involves going around in circles. The crooked line is not a straight line and the circle is not a straight line. The upright person rejects all the roundabout and devious ways by which a person tries to conceal his intention in order to achieve his aim in a subtle way. That is why he rejects the policy of the second and third reason which is used by some people who try to conceal the first reason or the main true reason by presenting secondary less important reasons, hoping that the second, third or fourth reason may be of interest to the listener, even though it has no connection with the main subject. He does so in order to obtain the listener's approval by one way or another. Although the second reason may be right, yet it is not the pure truth but used only as an artifice to deceive the listener. Exaggeration also, whether in evaluating matters, or in describing their benefits and -

disadvantages, which is used just to convince the listener, does not tie in with uprightness nor does it conform with the speaker's respect of his own conscience or the conscience of others.

Uprightness and Trust

The upright person is trusted by whoever communicates or converses with him. His uprightness gives an idea of his spirituality and devoutness. Uprightness is not just a social virtue but it is one of the characteristics of the spiritual path. We say this because some may live in the atmosphere of the ministry inside the church while they have kept with them some of the wrong worldly means by which they fulfil their church aims. They serve and use inside the service crooked means which might cause others to stumble.

The spiritual aspirant needs continually to accustom himself to uprightness whatever it may cost him and whatever effort he may expend for its sake, even if he thinks he will suffer financial loss because of his uprightness in his dealings and in his service. He has to reject any profit or benefit that may come through any crooked means, knowing that it is not from God. The eternal life of a person is more important than any worldly benefit, and his example as a son of God and member of the body of Christ necessitates that he be blameless before people. Thus his conscience will be content and people will trust him. We have to put before our eyes the example of our saintly Fathers and follow in their steps.

CHAPTER FIVE

Values and Commitment

Values and Spiritual Evaluation

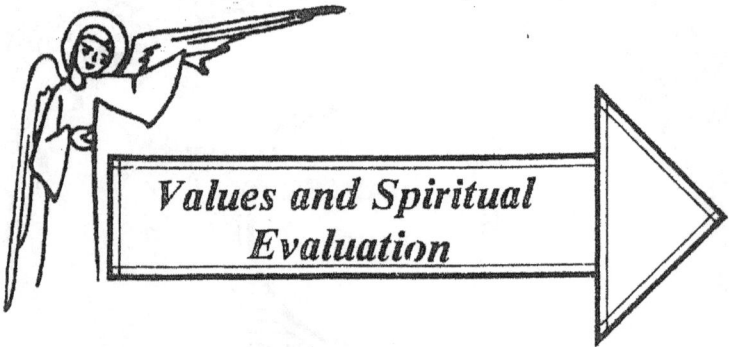

Values are the sublime invaluable matters which a person follows and which are adhered to as principles on commencing every deed.

What are the things of value in your opinion which direct you in life? People differ in values. The spiritual person has sublime values which he constantly sets before him, whilst others live in the world without values, or their values are other than spiritual, or they have their own valuation of matters according to which they follow a different aim and a different approach to life.

In the heart of every person is a certain concern which is of the utmost value in his opinion, for the sake of which he exerts every effort and on which he concentrates all his emotions. Some concentrate all their effort and values on wealth, others on fame and grandeur, whilst others on success and proficiency. According to this concentration, the sublime values may disappear or may not be thought of at all. Thus we encounter an important subject, namely, the aim and the means.

The Aim and the Means

A person may put before him a certain aim, giving it every value, no matter which means lead to it. For example, he may employ lies, deception, falsehood and cunning to attain the aim, whatever it may be. And if he fulfils his aim he relishes his success, even if he has walked over the dead bodies of others or if his comfort was based on the weariness of others in doing so. There is no doubt that such a person is a self-seeker, living without values, forfeiting both the aim and the means.

The spiritual aspirant, however, should set before him a good aim and his means to achieve this good aim should also be good. Such are those who have values and principles. Here we encounter another point: the meaning of success.

The Meaning of Success

Every person yearns to succeed. Success represents one of the values a person sets before him. **But what is success? We mean the true success** since evil-doers also rejoice when they succeed in achieving their sought-after evil and every person rejoices over the success of achieving his aim however improper the aim may be. This is not the success we mean.

Success is to overcome your own self, not to

overcome others.

Success is to attain purity of heart and not merely to achieve your aims whatever they may be.

Success is to achieve the kingdom of God in your heart and every other aim should be within this Kingdom. If your success is outside these values, then it is a failure and not a success. That is why a person may rejoice on earth whilst heaven laments his state. He may think that he has succeeded in something in the present world while he forfeits his eternal life. Here we ought to talk about an important value, namely, eternity.

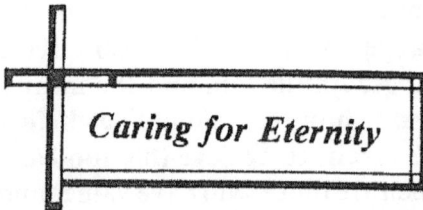

Caring for Eternity

The spiritual aspirant's prime concern is his eternity. He grows in this feeling until eternity occupies the whole of his concern, and his thoughts become focused on his eternal destiny. Eternity becomes of prime value in his life. Every deed or aim that conflicts with his eternal life is absolutely and unquestionably rejected. Therefore he considers his present life as mere preparation conducive to eternity. **His concern for eternity gives his present life a pure spiritual direction, keeping him steadfast in God and circumspect in His love and in keeping His commandments.**

This spiritual attitude is lacked by those who have made worldly positions and pleasures their prime value. Worldliness preoccupies them, overwhelming their thoughts and causing them to be oblivious of their eternal life. The Lord Jesus Christ presented us with a spiritual principle which we should set before our eyes on our spiritual path: *"For what is a man profited if he gains the whole world, and loses his own soul? Or what will a man give in exchange for his soul?"* (Matt.16:26).

Dear reader, may you ask yourself what value eternity has in your life? Is it one of the main values about which you are circumspect and of which you are always mindful? Or do you not think of it at all, being preoccupied with your various other concerns, forgetting the Lord's words to Martha: *"...you are worried and troubled about many things. But one thing is needed"* (Lk.10:41,42)?

What are the many things of this present world which demand of you more concern and consideration than your eternity? Has the time not come for you to rectify your spiritual criteria, revising your evaluation of matters so that eternity may take its due consideration and concentration in your heart, mind and time?

When we mention eternity, we mean your own eternal life and the eternal life of others. In other words, we mean your estimation of the importance of the kingdom of God within you and within all people. We mean the extent of your vigilance to enter this Kingdom together with everyone you know. Here it becomes obvious that the godlike zeal and the ministry constitute an important characteristic of the spiritual path and one of the values that lead your life.

The more the value of eternal life is elevated in your mind and in your heart, the less the value of the world becomes in your sight. Therefore, one of the characteristics of the spiritual life is not to appraise any of the matters of this present world, putting before you the Apostle's words: *"Do not love the world or the things* *in the world. If anyone loves the world, the love of the Father is not in him"* (1Jn.2:15).

Ask yourself frankly what is your assessment of the world? Is it your life, your enjoyment and your desire? Is it so attractive to the extent that you cannot do without its pleasures and entertainments, and would grieve if you departed it? Or are the world and all things in it mere rubbish to you as seen by Saint Paul the Apostle (Phil.3:8)? Solomon the Sage experienced the two conditions. He experienced looking at the world as a pleasure and said: *"Whatever my eyes desired I did not keep from them"* (Ecc.2:10), but when this world lost its value in his sight, he declared that *"all was vanity and grasping for the wind. There was no profit under the sun"* (Ecc.2:11).

According to your evaluation of the world will depend your dealing with it. Is the world trivial, vain and grasping for the wind? Or is it a passion attracting you vehemently: the lust of the flesh, the lust of the eyes, and the pride of life (1Jn.2:16)? May you, in your evaluation of the world, believe in its vanity and trust that it is passing away together with the lust of it (1Jn.2:17). Such are the values which you should believe in. Asceticism, mysticism, monasticism and celibacy sprang from belief in these values. Martyrdom itself was the fruit of belief in the value of eternal life and in the vanity of this world.

Saint Augustine experienced the various lusts of the world but when the world lost its value in his sight, he was able to say: "I found myself on top of the world when I felt within myself that I neither desire anything nor fear anything". Therefore if you want to lead a person to the love of God, you have to amend his criteria, his values and his outlook on matters. It was good, therefore, that the Apostle said: *"...be transformed by the renewing of your mind"* (Rom.12:2). What is the renewing of the mind other than changing its concepts and correcting its values so that its outlook on matters might be straightened and acquire a spiritual attitude?

Here we ask: What is your valuation of your spiritual and bodily needs?

The Spirit and the Body

There is no doubt that the majority of people give the whole or most of their concern to their body. They care for its nourishment and health, strength and beauty, providing it with its need of food, medicine and treatment, rest, activity and relaxation. In like manner they care for the bodies of their children and relatives. Yet their spirits do not take the same attention because the evaluation of the spirit's needs is never given a thought, or may be neglected. That is why people's spirits weaken, having received neither adequate spiritual nourishment nor care for the necessary spiritual fortifiers, practices and spiritual vitalizers such as reading and contemplation, psalmody and spiritual gatherings, prayer and ascetic practices.

The evaluation we give to the spirit defines our attitude to life. It induces us to care for the spiritual values and the spiritual means which help our spiritual growth and prompt us towards continual advancement along the spiritual path.

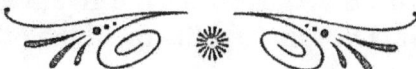

Examples of Spiritual Values

Prayer

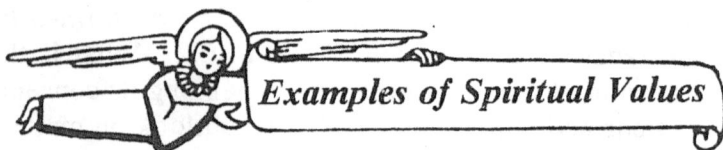

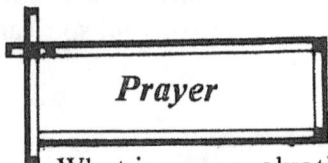

What is your evaluation of prayer? Is it a mere help to you in time of affliction, to which you turn when you need God? Or is it a statute, such that if you do not keep it your conscience reprimands you for the mere remissness? Or is it a necessary spiritual nourishment, such that if you do not take it your spiritual life suffers listlessness? Or is it an enjoyment in which you feel its sweet savour and during which you forget the world and all that is in it, wishing to prolong the time of your talk with God?

Your evaluation of prayer defines your spiritual level and your ability to continue in prayer. Therefore examine yourself regarding prayer, electing its befitting value. If you realise the true value of prayer, it will become for you, as the saints said, an integral part of you, indispensable like your breath. **Our failing sometimes is that we appraise human effort more than prayer!** That is why we prefer to depend on our striving, our intelligence and our experience more than on prayer. For such reasons we place prayer most of the time the last of our concerns. We pray if we find time to pray, or if we remember to pray, or when we are reminded to do so by others. **This is because we do not give prayer the value that befits it. The same applies to all the other spiritual**

practices.

Thus your whole life with God needs re-evaluation so that you may feel the importance of God to you and the importance of your life with Him. Then you will reorganise your life in the light of an ideal evaluation. If your life with God needs revaluation, so undoubtedly does your relationship with others.

Yourself and Others

What is your appreciation of man? Do you consider every man your brother in humanity? Do you love him, and is his concern your concern? Do you care for everyone, within your ability of course, as God cares for all? **Are you mindful of people's feelings? All people? Do you appraise the soul? Whoever's soul?** Is the soul of every person precious in your sight? Do you consider every man's soul as you would your own? Do you love every person as you love yourself, caring for him and his interests as you would the dearest of your friends, so that whatever befalls him befalls you, whatever gladdens him gladdens you, and whatever injures him injures you?

The esteem of the precious human soul, and the circumspection to observe the prerogatives and feelings of everyone is one of the values kept by the spiritual person.

My brother, if the value of man rises in your sight you will find yourself naturally respecting and loving everyone, not daring to hurt anyone's feelings, nor daring to err against or with any person causing them to stumble. You fear that God may request their blood from you in the Last Day.

I know that you care for the feelings of the elders. Yet you might neglect and ignore the lesser ones. But God is the God of all: He cares for the master as He cares for the slave. He cares for the elderly as well as the young, the sage as well as the uneducated. He shines His sun on the evildoers and the virtuous, and sends His rain on the righteous and the wicked. **No one is forgotten by God.** Every soul is dear to Him. He looks after the soul as the Good Shepherd who gives His life for His sheep (Jn.10). You should act in such a way because God left you a model.

If man has this value in your sight you will respect the freedom of others and you will respect their rights. You will not provoke anyone, nor plunder nor treat anyone unjustly, nor hurt nor pillory anyone but you will embrace all with your love.

The value of the human soul calls you to serve and to expend yourself for the sake of saving others. He who believes in the value of every soul, says with Saint Paul: *"Who is weak, and I am not weak? Who is made to stumble, and I do not burn with indignation?"* (2Cor.11:29), and remembers how the Lord went to look for the one soul which did not go unnoticed among the flock and did not lose its importance in the presence of the ninety-nine (Lk.15:4-7). He toils for the sake of the one single soul.

Comfort and Toil

The ordinary person is concerned with his own comfort even if it causes other people to suffer. But the person with values finds his true comfort when he toils for the sake of making others comfortable. To him comfort means to give comfort to others, not to himself. In his concept comfort is the comfort of his conscience and not the comfort of his body. He is fully aware that the true comfort is the eternal comfort and not the comfort on this earth and that **everyone in eternity will receive his reward according to his labour** (1Cor.3:8). That is why the toil for the sake of goodness is one of the values which the spiritual man cares for, and is one of the characteristics of the spiritual path.

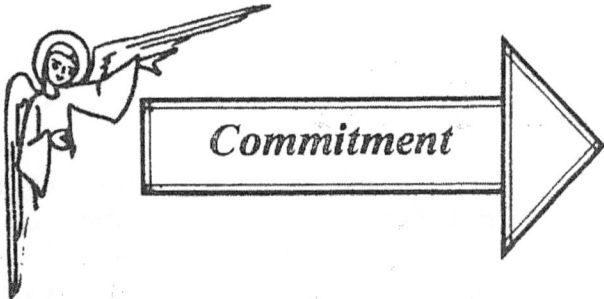

Commitment

Commitment is one of the most important characteristics of the spiritual path. He who does not adhere to his commitments is by no means spiritual. The spiritual person commits himself to every word he says and to every promise he makes, to every agreement with others and to every rule and covenant between him and God. He also abides by and follows particular principles and values, morals and spiritual rules. He lives responsibly. That is why he is respected by all. Any word he says has its weight and its importance to those he deals with. It is better than a written and authenticated agreement. Even if he does not speak but merely nods his head as a sign of approval, it is acknowledged that he is committed and will adhere to his agreement without the need for any witnesses or signatures. His commitment is proof of his manliness, of his respect to his word and of his respect to his promises and agreements. It is an honourable conduct. He is committed to what he decrees and to what he imposes on himself. He is also committed to the spiritual principles and to what is imposed on him by the general discipline and principles. He also feels that he is committed in his relationship with God, to obey Him and keep His commandments.

The Holy Bible gives us wonderful examples of the

virtue of commitment. Abraham the Patriarch held fast to the life of obedience. He carried it out despite all the hardships it entailed. He obeyed God when he was called to leave his relatives and his land and to walk after Him without knowing where he was going (Heb.11:8). His commitment reached its sublimity when he offered his only son- for whose sake he had received all the promises- as a burnt offering. Jephthah the Gileadite was an example of commitment. He made a vow to God, and though carrying it out was beyond human capability he carried it out in respect for his vow to the Lord (Judg.11:34,35).

Contrary to Abraham and Jephthah was Samson who did not abide by his vow so he forfeited his soul, lost his strength, was taken captive by his enemies, and became a maxim (Judg.16).

Commitment to Covenants, Vows and Oaths

The spiritual person is committed to his covenants with the Lord. Have you fulfilled all your covenants with God? The first covenant between you and God was your pledge on the day of your baptism to renounce Satan and all his intrigues, all his evil, all his unclean spirits and all his wicked deeds. Do you still adhere to this pledge in practice? In every repentance and confession, you undertake before God to abandon sin without return. Do you abide by this? In every Holy Communion, you undertake many promises. Do you remember them? Have you carried them out? Or have you not adhered to them?

How many times have you suffered severe affliction and undertaken before God that if He saves you, you will do such and such? Do you abide by all the pledges which you undertook before God during your affliction? Behold David the Prophet says: *"I will pay my vows to the Lord now in the presence of all His people"* (Ps.116:14,18). Are you like him? Are you devoted to all your vows or do you, after vowing, retreat and change your mind, or postpone paying your vow, or change or disregard it? Do you commit yourself to what you say in your prayers? In every prayer you say: *"Forgive us our trespasses as we forgive those who trespass against us"*. Do you truly forgive others as you say or do you not commit yourself to the words you pray? Review what you say in your prayers, put them into practice, and see where you stand. How many New Year Eves have passed in which you stood before God making vows and promises? And on how many holy occasions have you stood before God praying and in how many spiritual moments has your heart burnt with repentance and you made promises and vows to God, but you adhered to none of them

Lack of Commitment

Lack of commitment involves a type of indifference and licence of behaviour, and detachment from every bond, condition and agreement in a disrespectful manner. Absence of commitment means that a person is devoid of the sense of responsibility and seriousness, and is proof of weakness.

Lack of commitment appeared from the beginning of creation. Our fathers did not adhere to the commandment they received from God and He drove them out of Paradise, and we have seen the adversities which have befallen mankind due to their failure to adhere to their commitment. The children of Israel also failed in their commitment to the farthest extent. When Moses presented them with the ten commandments of God, they all cried out to him, saying: *"...tell us all that the Lord our God says to you, and we will hear and do it"* (Deut.5:27). Were they dedicated to this pledge? Or did they, after a while, worship the golden calf (Ex.32)? Has any generation of mankind adhered to this declaration? How wonderful is the saying of David the Prophet: *"Accept, I pray, the freewill offerings of my mouth, O Lord"* (Ps.119:108)! When you pray these words, do you mean them? Do you mean what you are saying, which is: "Give me, O Lord, a spirit of commitment that I may carry out all my pledges and not break my vows"?

If we have to carry out our agreements with people in a spirit of commitment, how much more should we be committed in our agreements with God? He who does not commit himself tries to cover his failure to adhere with many excuses, reasons and pretexts in order to evade his responsibility. He often gives excuses of hindrances and obstacles, or that the matter was beyond his will and ability, or that the circumstances were unfavourable, or that he had forgotten, or that he had no time or was unable. In most cases the true reason is that he is not used to the life of commitment and to respecting his word. The spiritual person, however, commits himself and exerts every effort to overcome every obstacle. He fulfils his commitments whatever happens, irrespective of the difficulties he may encounter, as a responsible person. He despises himself if he presents an excuse to be exempted from his commitment.

That is why you feel comfortable when you deal with someone who has a sense of commitment. If you agree with him on something, rest assured that you are walking on safe ground which will inevitably produce sound results. In working with someone who adheres to his commitments you sleep restful, confident that you are working with a man who appreciates the situation and respects his agreements.

He who does not commit himself follows his whims, not heeding orders or regulations, trying to loosen himself from everything he deems restrictive. He does not fulfil his commitments either in his worldly life or in his spiritual life. He may refuse to succumb to any general rule, feeling that this is his personal freedom, even though this freedom breaks in its path regulations and rules. This is why he does not comprehend the true meaning of freedom. He thinks that freedom is a type of licence binding him to nothing. He believes that regulations are restrictions constraining his opinion and his will. True freedom, however, is to be free from the lusts, passions and bad habits that enslave him. When he detaches himself from commitment in the name of freedom, society is obliged to compel him. So he abandons commitment and faces compulsion. Thus he confronts law and punishment and needs supervision by society as well as inspection, following up and control. If he persists in his non-adherence, he will be exposed to punishments and compelled unwillingly to fulfil his commitment. His obedience is submission to compulsion and not love for commitment.

Nevertheless, in the Church and spiritual environment, for the sake of dispute and love of controversy, some may ask: What is the need for commitment when we are under grace and not under the law?

Grace does not conflict with commitment. He who through grace has risen above the level of the law's requirements is not required to submit to the law but he who is below that is. An example of this is paying the tithes. You are not bound by the law of the tithes if you pay more, conforming to the principles: *"Give to him who asks you, and from him who wants to borrow from you do not turn away"* and *"sell your possessions and give to the poor"*. This is the level of grace. If you have not attained to it you are committed to the law of tithes. Also some may object to the seven daily prayers. If you have been elevated above this level and reached the continual prayer or praying always or your life has become a prayer, your question may be subject to discussion. But if you are at a much lower level than the seven daily prayers, you are undoubtedly committed to reciting them and they will teach you continual prayer.

May we all, brethren, live the life of commitment because it embraces within it the life of obedience and the life of humility. It also includes seriousness, meticulousness and the fear of God, because all virtues are connected with each other.

Qualities of the Committed Person

The committed person respects himself, his word, his promises and his relations with people. His commitment engenders trust in him, in his work and in his behaviour. He is appreciated by all, as they realize that they can depend on him, trust his word and co-operate with him because he is the sort of person who can withstand obstacles and overcome hindrances even if this causes him self-constraint and forbearance in order to carry out what was commended to him. Not only does he commit himself to carrying out the work but also to performing it proficiently. This is why he is always successful and feels that his work, his efficiency and his success are part of his conscience, honour and self-respect. He cares for all these, feeling that any remissness causes embarrassment to him and to everyone who co-operates and works with him.

Outside his working environment, the committed person adheres to his commitments in his private life and in his spiritual life. He abides by every spiritual practice which he lays down for himself or which is laid down by his spiritual father. He commits himself to all his ascetic practices. He also commits himself to the system of his prayer, fasting, prostrations and spiritual readings. He does not swerve from them or lessen them or present excuses to justify his failings. He does not find in the external circumstances a justification for his non-adherence. Therefore the committed person is always an example and a lesson to others to learn seriousness in life. This is contrary to the one who does not commit himself who is a bad example causing others to stumble when imitating him.

He who commits himself is vigilant over all his energy in order that he may be able to fulfil his commitments. He is cautious over his time because he is committed to a ministry or appointments and he is not used to falling short in them. He is careful with his time to use it in perfecting the work he is committed to perform. He does not waste his efforts nor his energy nor his time in trivial matters that may crop up nor in amusements, else he would be unable to fulfil his commitments.

He who commits himself always reminds himself so as not to forget any of his commitments. He does not believe in forgetfulness as an excuse to justify his omissions. That is why he records in his diary all his responsibilities and frequently reads it to avoid forgetfulness. He also behaves in his service with the spirit of commitment which is an attribute of every successful minister. He abides by the time of his service, he does not arrive late or forget it. He abides by the programme and does not innovate a special one for himself. He does not fail to adhere to preparing the lesson, making it rich and satisfying to his listeners. He does not omit preparing it with the pretext that he already knows it. He also commits himself to the meeting of servers and to the discipline of the service in every respect.

The spiritual minister also commits himself to time. If he is invited to give a sermon for one hour he does not take two hours, unheeding the time of the congregation and their private appointments. He also adheres to the subject of the sermon. He does not waste the time in side issues which have no relation with the main subject. Thus the minister who commits himself is meticulous in everything, in time and in the subject matter.

Commitment is an important element in the life of pastors and clergymen. They are committed to perform all their church responsibilities with regard to rituals, visitations to all the congregation, appointments for confession, and to visiting hospitals and the sorrowful. They are also committed to their responsibilities towards the poor and the needy, presenting themselves as ideals in every virtue. The pastor who does not commit himself does not see before him a definite duty he has to perform. In his service he does whatever appears pleasing in his eyes, adhering to nothing, following no plan or discipline.

Commitment also comes in the realm of doctrine and dogma. Every person who stands at the pulpit to teach should adhere to the teachings of the Holy Bible and the doctrine of the Church. He should not present his listeners with his personal opinions or beliefs, or what he was able to collect from his own readings but he should act what the Holy Bible says and what has reached the Church through Tradition. To this effect Saint Paul says to his disciple Bishop Timothy: *"And the things that you have heard from me among many witnesses, commit these to faithful men who will be able to teach others also"* (2Tim.2:2).

For this reason the spiritual person is also bound to the teaching of the Church, to her regulations, rituals, fasts, prayers and all her canons. He should not walk in one direction and the whole Church in another, because in the commitment of all there is oneness of heart and of thought, of worship and of faith. That is why the life of humility befits the life of commitment because the humble person submits to regulations whereas the haughty interprets matters according to his own understanding.

CHAPTER SIX

Wisdom and Discernment

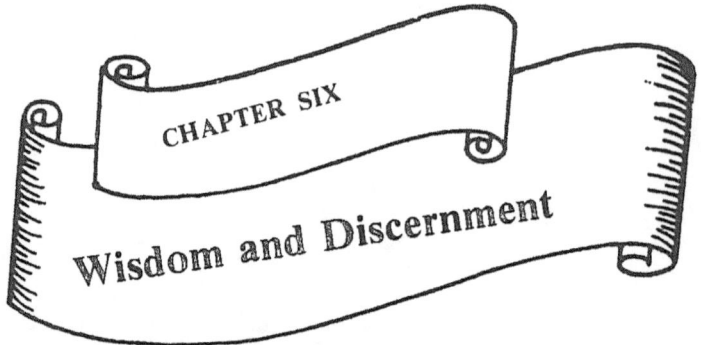

Wisdom and Discernment

The Importance of Wisdom and Discernment

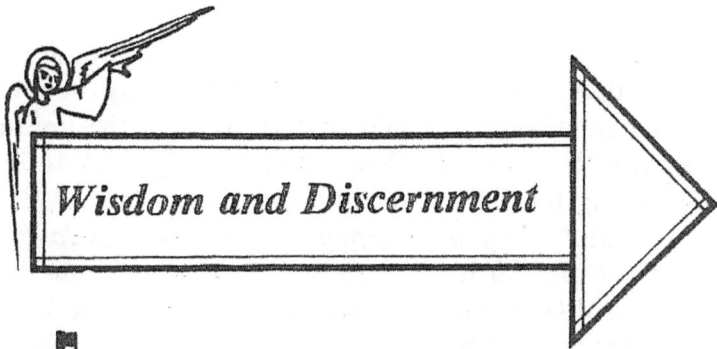

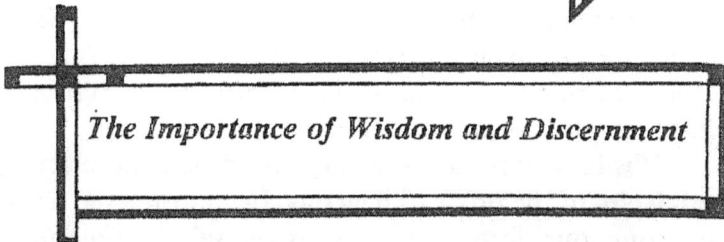

When saint Abba Antony the Great, the father of monks, was asked: "Which is the greatest of all virtues?", he answered, "Discernment is undoubtedly the greatest". Discernment means that a person discriminates between right and wrong and distinguishes between good and evil.

Many people observe fasts, prayers, confession, partaking of the Holy Communion and reading the Holy Bible, yet they fail in their spiritual life because they have no discernment, that is, they practise all these things without any wisdom, without any understanding and without discrimination.

The person should practise every virtue with wisdom. He should first understand the meaning and essence of the virtue and know how and when to practise it. Thus discernment permeates every virtue. The Holy Bible says: *"The wise man's eyes are in his head, but the*

108

fool walks in darkness" (Ecc.2:14). The Lord Jesus Christ drew people's attention to wisdom many times to the extent that it was said that He praised the unjust steward because he had dealt wisely (Lk.16:8). Regarding the importance of walking in wisdom, the Lord said: *"...be wise as serpents and harmless as doves"* (Matt.10:16). Such was the wise conduct of all the children of God in life and in ministry. We see that Saint Peter the Apostle praised the wisdom with which Saint Paul the Apostle preached, saying: *"...as also our beloved brother Paul, according to the wisdom given to him, has written to you"* (2Pet.3:15).

Wisdom was a necessary condition in electing ministers to the order of deacons. In choosing the seven deacons our fathers the Apostles said: *"Therefore, brethren, seek out from among you seven men of good reputation, full of the Holy Spirit and wisdom, whom we may appoint over this business"* (Acts 6:3).

Wisdom Is One of the Names of Christ

Owing to its importance, wisdom is one of the titles of the Second Person of the Holy Trinity. The Apostle speaks of Christ the Lord, saying that He is *"the power of God and the wisdom of God,"* (1Cor.1:24) *"in whom are hidden all the treasures of wisdom and knowledge"* (Col.2:3). And it is written in the Book of Proverbs: *"Wisdom has built her house, she has hewn out her seven pillars"* (Prov.9:1), that is, the Seven Sacraments of the Church.

Wisdom and the Holy Spirit

He in whom the Spirit of God dwells is no doubt a dwelling place for wisdom also. It is said of the Holy Spirit in the Book of Isaiah the Prophet that He is the Spirit of the Lord, the Spirit of wisdom, the Spirit of understanding and the Spirit of counsel (Is.11:2). And Saint Paul said to the Ephesians that the Holy Spirit is *"the Spirit of wisdom and revelation in the knowledge of Him"*, Whom, if they received, would enlighten the eyes of their understanding (Eph.1:17,18). The Apostle also mentioned that wisdom is one of the gifts of the Holy Spirit (1Cor.12:8).

The Wisdom of God and the Wisdom of the World

We discriminate between the wisdom of God and the cunning of the world as it is said that God *"catches the wise in their own craftiness"* (1Cor.3:19). Saint Paul explained in detail the difference between the wisdom of God and the wisdom of the world which will be destroyed (1Cor.1:19), and said that *"the wisdom of this world is foolishness with God"* (1Cor.3:19), and called it *"the wisdom of men"* (1Cor.2:5), the wisdom *"according to the flesh"* (1Cor.1:26) and *"the wisdom of this age"* (1Cor.2:6), and added that *"God has chosen the foolish things of the world to put to shame the wise"* (1Cor.1:27).

The Apostle talked about the spiritual wisdom which is from God and His Spirit, saying: *"However, we speak wisdom among those who are mature, yet not the wisdom of this age, nor of the rulers of this age, who are coming to nothing. But we speak the wisdom of God in a mystery, the hidden wisdom which God ordained before the ages for our glory"* (1Cor.2:6,7). **And of this wisdom which is from God, Saint James the Apostle said that it is the wisdom which is *"from above"* and explained it in detail,** saying: *"But the wisdom that is from above is first pure, then peaceable, gentle, willing to yield, full of mercy and good fruits, without partiality and without hypocrisy"* (Jas.3:17). He differentiated between this wisdom and the wisdom of the world which he described as *"earthly, sensual, demonic"* (Jas.3:15), saying that from it come *"envy and self-seeking..., confusion and every evil thing"* (Jas.3:16).

The wisdom of the world is full of craftiness and cunning. Its means are lies and deception and it has many openings from which Satan enters. In this manner the serpent, which was *"more cunning than any beast of the field"* (Gen.3:1), behaved when she deceived our mother Eve. And Jezebel the wife of the evil King Ahab behaved similarly when she contrived an unlawful scheme for her husband to possess the vineyard of Naboth the Jezreelite (1Kin.21:5-15).

Likewise our mother Rebekah behaved with worldly wisdom in order to obtain for her son Jacob the blessing

of his father. It was through lies, deception and cunning that even Jacob feared and said to her: *"I shall bring a curse on myself and not a blessing"* (Gen.27:12).

Not every means employed to fulfil your aim is a sound means. **It is surprising that worldly ways often fulfil the aim more quickly. Nevertheless, they are not acceptable to God.** Our father Abraham took Keturah to wife and she begot Zimran, Jokshan, Medan, Midian, Ishbak, and Shuah who gave birth to Sheba, Dedan, Asshurim, Letushim, and Leummim and others (Gen.25:1-4). These children were not accepted before God. It was a quick way for Abraham to have children but it was through human means and was unacceptable before God.

Another example of human wisdom which was not acceptable to God was the counsel of Ahithophel. It was human intelligence which brought about a result but it was an evil intelligence, and the virtuous pray the Lord to deliver them from it (2Sam.15:31). Likewise was the counsel which Balaam presented to Balak (Rev.2:14). **This is the deception of the devil by which he misleads the world in every generation and will mislead people in the last age.**

It is intelligence, knowledge and cunning which produces an outcome, or it is a diabolic wisdom as mentioned by our teacher Saint James the Apostle (Jas.3:15).

We have to keep away from all these matters and reject their outcome even if they seem to be favourable for us. Whatever the devil presents to us and whatever our intelligence presents to us of thought which may seem to be good, let us reject them if the means are unsound and unspiritual. The Holy Bible warns us, saying: *"There is a way that seems right to a man, but its end is the way of death"* (Prov.14:12); (Prov.16:25).

Sources of Wisdom

The first source of wisdom is God. The wisdom from God is gained through prayer, according to the Apostle's words: ***"If any of you lacks wisdom, let him ask of God, who gives to all liberally and without reproach, and it will be given to him. But let him ask in faith, with no doubting"*** (Jas.1:5,6). Thus we continually pray to God to guide us, we pray to Him to enlighten our minds and our hearts, to inspire us with wisdom and teach us how to walk in His path. As long as wisdom is from above, let us then seek it from above.

The second source of wisdom is seeking counsel from people on whose mouths God talks. Concerning this the Apostle Saint Paul says: *"Remember those who rule over you, who have spoken the word of God to you, whose faith follow... Obey those who rule over you, and be submissive, for they watch out for your souls, as those who must give account"* (Heb.13:7-17). How truthful is the beautiful verse which says that those who have no guide fall like the leaves of the tree!

The third source of wisdom is the wise and the experienced. Seeking counsel is not sufficient but with counselling there must be submission and obedience. You have to choose a wise spiritual counsellor from whom you can assimilate wisdom. **Saint Antony, at the beginning of his monastic life when he was seeking**

counsel from the ascetics, was like the bee which sucks nectar from every flower. Many are those who seek wisdom from one person and become a carbon copy of them, but Saint Antony learnt mysticism from one person, prayer from another, meekness of heart from a third, cheerfulness from a fourth, knowledge from a fifth, and so on.

The Most Important Domain Where Wisdom Is Necessary

In fact deeds are divided into four categories. The first category of deeds are those which are obviously good. The second category are those which are explicitly evil. And these two need no discrimination. **The third type needs reasoning whether the deed is right or wrong. The person is unsure of its means and outcomes.** In this matter he needs wisdom and discernment or at least some good advice and a word of benefit to enlighten the way before him. Here appears the need for spiritual fathers, counsellors and the sage. **The fourth kind of deed which also needs wisdom and discernment is the preference between two ways where the conscience does not know which of the two is better.** The two ways may be good but which is better and which is more suitable for the person is not clear. An example of this is when a person does not know whether to choose the monastic life or the ministry of Priesthood. **Both of them are good, but which is better or more suitable for the person?** Such matters need wisdom, discernment and time until the person examines himself and hears the voice of God in his heart or through the mouth of a wise father or a sincere counsellor. The matter needs wisdom within us or within our counsellors.

Another domain where wisdom and discrimination are needed is the way of acquiring and advancing in a virtue. The virtues are clear; they are explained in the spiritual books. But what is the starting point and what is the ideal way to acquire them? Some may rush into a virtue and end in a reverse result or a spiritual relapse. Others may walk slowly and end in slackness, listlessness and slothfulness. **The mind may stand at a loss between the fervour of hastiness and the slowness of the gradual approach and it needs wisdom to know how to behave.**

To reply that hastiness is better or that slowness is better is not a sound reply. When there is a strong spur of grace or a spark of the Holy Spirit, then there should not be halting. This is what happened with Saint Abba Mishael the hermit and Saints Maximos and Domadius and the like who attained quickly, but in other cases the gradual walk is more suitable.

Discernment is also necessary in sensitive matters connected with a person's destiny. A person may act ignorantly and regret it all his life. He may commit an error which would be the error of his whole life over which he laments his whole life long, and weeping avails him nothing. The matter needs vigilance, wisdom or counselling.

Sometimes a person is enthusiastic in taking a certain attitude which overwhelms all his emotions but would prove not in his favour, and he may regret it afterwards. He may say when the matter is irreversible: "I wish I had not done that. I wish I had waited and taken counsel or listened to the advice which I rejected vigorously". The matter may have needed discernment in many other angles of the subject or in certain outcomes. **That is why counselling gives other opinions, insight into some unclear angles and perception of some overlooked outcomes.**

There is another essential point which needs discernment and wisdom. It is centred on the sound conception of some virtues which gives them integrity with the other virtues, away from excessiveness.

Wisdom Confers Sound Conception

Many times a person comes and says: "I dealt with people with humbleness and forgiveness and the result was that I suffered and became despised among them". **Here the defect is not in the life of humility but in practising it without discernment and without understanding.** Such a person needs to comprehend the true meaning of humility and how it should be; how humility should be in wisdom and discernment, so that it would not lead to such distress or to any bad result, but be fixed in the heart. **After having this bad experience, such a person may revert, hate humility, walk in violence and cling to self-dignity.**

No doubt there are many virtues which if the person practises without discernment would lead to unexpected results and may cause the spiritual life to end in apostasy, reversed deviation and a psychological complex. The reason is practising the virtue without discernment and without wisdom, or in extremity and rashness.

That is why employing the contents of *The Lives of the Desert Fathers'*, various other spiritual books and discourses on the high spiritual levels and ideals, need counselling, discernment and wisdom. **Do not read about a virtue which the saints might have acquired over tens of years of striving and which you decide to carry out there and then to the same high level without assimilation, discernment and wisdom.** This advice covers many virtues, such as:

1. Silence and solitude
2. Fasting, abstinence and successive abstinence for days
3. Humility and taking the last seat
4. Tears and contrition of heart
5. The meaning of cheerfulness and dejection
6. Continual prayer
7. The meaning of judging and counselling
8. Meekness and the strong personality
9. Forgiveness, strictness and chastening
10. Mysticism, asceticism and possessionlessness
11. Defending the Truth
12. Obedience and purity of conscience

Intelligence and Wisdom

The true wisdom is the wisdom which comes from above as one of the gifts of the Holy Spirit. It is completely different from human or worldly wisdom alleged by some and which is not from God. Some people possess shrewdness, tactfulness and diplomacy which they think of as wisdom, and some have cleverness and intelligence which they regard as wisdom! All these may be completely remote from the true wisdom which comes from above. Here we would like to differentiate between intelligence and wisdom.

Wisdom has a much wider meaning than intelligence. Intelligence may be a mere part of wisdom. A person may enjoy an extraordinary intelligence and an excellent intellect, yet he does not behave wisely. There may be obstacles which hinder his thinking and intelligence in his practical life. He may be obsessed by a certain lust which governs his behaviour so he completely succumbs to it and behaves without wisdom despite his intelligence which may have been impeded by the lust which took over the reins. In his behaviour he may submit to nervous outbreaks and behave with his nerves instead of his intelligence and thence his behaviour would lack wisdom. He may have intelligence but fall short in experience and knowledge. Thus his inadequacy leads him to unwise behaviour.

What then is wisdom? And how is it different from intelligence?

The source of intelligence is the reason. And

intelligence can be merely a sound intellectual activity. But wisdom does not depend on the mind alone. It benefits from experience, counselling, prayer and the direction of the Holy Spirit. It is manifested in good behaviour following sound reasoning. Therefore wisdom is not just the right knowledge or the mere proper reasoning but it is involved in the core of practical life, expressing its existence in good behaviour. It is not mere theoretical or intellectual information.

How true are the words of Saint James the Apostle: *"Who is wise and understanding among you? Let him show by good conduct that his works are done in the meekness of wisdom"* (Jas.3:13). Indeed, sound reasoning or intelligence enters a thorough test in practical situations. If it succeeds, it will become wisdom.

A person may be intelligent and think rightly but lack precision in expressing himself due to his lack of knowledge of the proper meaning of words. But the wise person says what he means and means what he says. Thus wisdom comprises good reasoning, accurate expression and sound behaviour. Here we say that every wise person is intelligent but not every intelligent person is wise. If the wise person lacks intelligence he compensates for it by obtaining counsel, reading and benefiting from his own and others' experiences.

Due to the importance of experience in wisdom, we hear the term *'the wisdom of the elderly'* which means that during their lifetime the elderly gained various experiences giving them wisdom irrespective of their level of intelligence, because intelligence is not everything in life.

The wise counsellors add sound reasoning to the

minds of those whom they counsel. They give new points of view which have gone unnoticed due to the lack of experience and limited perception of their disciples, thus preventing them from acting rashly because of a certain desire in the heart. **Here we see that rashness hinders intelligence or pushes it towards a certain direction.** That is why, however intelligent you are, remember the words of the Holy Bible: *"...lean not on your own understanding"* (Prov.3:5). Your understanding centres within a limited frame which is your own knowledge, experience and outlook, and it does you no harm to add to it other outlooks, knowledge and experience through enquiring or counselling.

The wise person is not rash in his conduct but he withholds his own opinion until he attains to a deeper and wider perception.

Hindrances to Wisdom

One of the hindrances to wisdom is hastiness in conduct. That is why the wise are described as being discreet. Hastiness does not allow for sound thinking, scrutinizing and knowing other opinions, nor does it give a chance to seek counsel or the guidance of God through prayer. **It entails a type of superficiality. Hasty behaviour is often frivolous and chaotic.** God may send to the hasty person someone to advise him, saying: "Be on your guard. Take heed to yourself. Give yourself a chance to think. Revise the matter with yourself".

Regarding this, we mention how some of our children in the diaspora come to Egypt desiring to get married within a couple of weeks. Contrary to this was Saint Makarios the Great. When he had a thought of going into the inner wilderness to see the hermit fathers, we find him saying: "I kept fighting this thought for three years to see whether it was from God or not".

The conduct of the wise is prudent and discreet, taking its due of thinking, profound study and scrutiny, even if they are accused of being slow.

We do not deny that some matters need speediness but there is a difference between speediness and rashness. Rashness is the hastiness which is void of study and scrutiny. It is perilous if connected with essential matters or destinies. That is why I always say: **The right solution is not the fast solution but the perfect solution.**

Hastiness may be a quality of the youth because they are enthusiastic and want matters to be done promptly. However, if they study the matter with their elders they may be convinced by them that hastiness has its dangers. Hastiness may be a natural quality of some people. They need to train themselves on thinking and reflection.

A person often regrets a hasty action which causes him to err or to treat anyone unjustly. An example of this is the reporter who hastens to publish a news item in order to gain a scoop, then it is proven that the news was incorrect and the reporter makes people lose their trust in the accuracy of the news. Another example is the father who punishes his child, or the superior who punishes his subordinates for some error, when it is later proven that they were innocent.

Another hindrance to wisdom is misunderstanding or lack of knowledge. Despite being very intelligent a man might be a failure in his married life. The reason of his failure may be his lack of knowledge of the psychology of the woman. He treats her as he treats men. The wise person would study the mentality, psychology and circumstances of the woman so as to deal with her wisely. In the same way the woman should study the psychology of the man and his mentality so as to understand how to deal with him wisely.

We say the same about treating children. We should study the psychology of the child and his mentality so as to know how to treat him wisely. This is also needed in dealing with people in general. That is why everyone should study the psychology, mentality and circumstances of the people with whom he deals whether colleagues at work or superiors or subordinates or friends or neighbours, so that he can treat them in the way that suits them.

If you study the psychology and mentality of the people you deal with, you will know the keys by which you can enter their heart and thus you will succeed in your dealings with them. Even if the keys go wrong you will know how to lubricate them and try again to open the door and it will open.

It is true that sometimes our failure in dealing with certain persons is due more to our lack of knowledge of the way to treat them than to defects in them. That is why we need to study some of the points about dealing with people.

Wisdom in Whether or not to Keep Silence

Silence is a well known practice among young persons. By it they try to get rid of the errors of the tongue, following the words of the Holy Book: *"In the multitude of words sin is not lacking, but he who restrains his lips is wise"* (Prov.10:19), and the words of David the Prophet: *"Set a guard, O Lord, over my mouth; keep watch over the door of my lips"* (Ps.141:3), and also following the words of the great Saint Arsenius: "Many times have I spoken and regretted but I have never regretted my silence".

Nevertheless the wise person knows that not every silence is a virtue nor every speech a sin. The wise person does not keep silent when he should speak and does not speak when he should keep silent. In wisdom he knows when to speak and how to speak. If he speaks he knows how far he should talk and the manner of his speech, and the words: *"Your lips, O my spouse, drip as honeycomb; honey and milk are under your tongue,"* (Song 4:11) apply to him. He utters beneficial words and words of comfort and of wisdom. Everyone feels that it was not him who spoke but the Spirit of his Father who speaks in him (Matt.10:20). **Thus he speaks cautiously, reflectively, wisely and beneficially and does not regret any word he says and does not long for the silence which protects him from the errors of the tongue.**

The problem, therefore, needs discernment, and silence should not be taken as an ascetic practice in a literal way void of Spirit because in some cases, silence may have errors.

The wise person knows well how to behave when he faces the foolishness of people, whereas the ordinary person finds himself bewildered before two verses: *"Do not answer a fool according to his folly, lest you also be like him"* (Prov.26:4), and: *"Answer a fool according to his folly, lest he be wise in his own eyes"* (Prov.26:5). There is no contradiction between these two verses. By wisdom man perceives when to answer the fool and when not to answer him. If your answer makes you equal to him it is better for you to keep silent and not to answer him, but if your silence makes him wise in his own eyes it is better to reveal to him the foolishness of his words.

Wisdom is the deciding factor in the matter and through discernment you discriminate which of the two ways is better. It is ignorance to give one rule for all cases. We cannot say to you that you should keep silence when one word from you would solve a problem nor can we say that you should speak in all circumstances.

A person should not read what is recorded in *'The Lives of the Desert Fathers'* and apply it to himself literally without seeking advice when he is not a monk and his spiritual circumstances are different from those of monks.

Sometimes silence can be discretion, wisdom, avoidance of errors and problems and it can also be a realm of contemplation and prayer. In other cases it may be ignorance, laziness or foolishness. It may be fear or unmanly behaviour. Through discernment you can discriminate between every case. A spiritual counsellor

124

should not put his disciple under a law, restrained by commandments whose aims he cannot perceive, but he should give his disciple wisdom and discernment and leave him to behave in every case as he deems fit. What we say about silence applies also to the other virtues.

Wisdom in Dejection and Cheerfulness

Some youth start their spiritual life with repentance and weeping over their sins as written in 'The Lives of the Desert Fathers', putting before them the verse which says: *"For by a sad countenance the heart is made better"* (Ecc.7:3). They continue in this state to the extent that the sadness of their countenance becomes a fixed feature of them and the regime of their life, remembering how the Lord gave the blessedness to those who mourn (Matt.5:4). They put before them the virtue of tears which springs from contrition of heart. **And tears can be a sign of repentance, an indication of tender feelings and sensitivity, and having fruits of mysticism and mortification to the world.** Nevertheless the person who walks in it needs thorough discernment lest the matter leads him to the contrary. This is because continuity of sadness of countenance and lack of wisdom in walking in it may lead to many errors.

How easy it is for the continuous dejection to turn into a stumbling block causing fear to those who wish to approach the life with God. They see that religious life is but weeping and dejection. This is a distorted picture about the life with God, which God willed to be continuous joy, as the Apostle said: *"Rejoice in the Lord always. Again I will say, rejoice!"* (Phil.4:4), mentioning that joy is a fruit of the Holy Spirit (Gal.5:22).

The continuity of gloominess may be used by the devil to throw the person into despair, loss of hope, despondency and weakening of morals. Dejection may also generate boredom and resentment.

The wise person knows the extent of contrition and tears, and knows how to mingle them with hope and solace, and knows how to live the life of joy in his repentance, contrition and tears. His tears which are shed in secret, are comforting tears and not burning tears. The matter needs wisdom because religion is not literal and not mere ambiguous virtues but it is Spirit and life. Therefore he who walks in contrition and tears should walk in wisdom. He who walks in the life of joy should also walk in wisdom lest he is led to indifference and carelessness.

Sometimes people benefit from your tears when they see that you are a spiritual person caring for your salvation and having tender feelings. But at other times when you have a sad countenance you might make people worry and question. **That is why many spiritual leaders keep their tears to their private life and appear smiling before people.** They do this out of their care for people's feelings lest by their worry they make them worry, and also to make others joyful even when they are sad. I was much pleased with the words of the writer who said: **"How noble is the sad heart when it hides its sadness to sing a song with the delighted hearts".** That is why it is not wise that a person lays down for himself a spiritual practice and carries it out without discernment, heedless of the surrounding circumstances because this leads to many problems.

The wise person does not take one verse from the Holy Bible and apply it to his life literally. He knows when to use the verse in its good season and when to add to it other verses to clarify its meaning.

Discernment in the Spiritual Practices

The spiritual life is not just constraints, laws and statutes, but it is the spirit's abiding in God with love and freedom. For example a person lays down a rule for himself not to laugh this week because laughter leads him to listlessness. Then arises a happy occasion in which he remains unsmiling and rigid and this may spoil his relationship with others. Will he call this steadfastness in the practice or is it lack of discrimination?

The spiritual practice should not be dry, literal and void of understanding. Spiritual practices are not restraints and chains. He who walks wisely in the sound spiritual life knows how to do one thing for the sake of God and how to do exactly the opposite for the sake of God also. So, for every situation there is what suits it. And our teacher Saint Paul says about his own practices in matters and their opposites: *"Everywhere and in all things I have learned both to be full and to be hungry, both to abound and to suffer need"* (Phil.4:12). The children of God take the Spirit of life and not verses and letters. They know when to do one thing and when to do its opposite with a clear conscience as the Holy Bible says: *"Rejoice with those who rejoice, and weep with those who weep"* (Rom.12:15). **Then everything under the heavens has its own time, as the Book of Ecclesiastes says, a time for weeping, a time for laughter, a time for keeping silence and a time for speaking** (Ecc.3:1-8).

It is good that everything is done in its season in the way that befits it, with wisdom. The wise person does the suitable thing in the appropriate time without constraining himself to a certain condition that continues with him all his life.

Discernment in Reading and Applying

Some people read and apply what they read literally. Then they suffer and in most cases they relapse. An example is someone who reads *'The Lives of the Desert Fathers'* and applies literally what he reads, oblivious of two things:

1. **The book records high levels attained by the saintly Fathers after long periods of striving, and these levels are not for beginners.**

2. **The book records recommendations given by the Fathers to certain persons whose circumstances are different from their own.**

Sometimes the saintly father might have given one person a certain advice and given another person different advice as he deemed fit for him. The saints did not give the same advice to everyone. As for us, we have to select from all the advice what suits us and apply it by degrees.

We say the same thing about the psalms. Some of the psalms are suitable for joy and some are suitable for mourning. You take what suits you when you apply them to yourself. Some of the psalms are of a high level which you may not have attained but you pray them as patterns set before you. The same applies to every spiritual book you read. You have to put before you two things:

1. The spirit of the words and not the letter, and

2. What suits you personally. By this I mean what suits your circumstances and your level, what suits your spiritual stature, and what suits your capacity and capabilities, in addition to what conforms with your gradual walk in God's path.

It is very dangerous to apply what you read without discernment, wisdom and guidance. We seek the peaceful spiritual life which grows, loves and walks in goodness wisely.

The Example of Kindness and Strictness

Some people use kindness or meekness only. Others prefer strictness and violent behaviour as a way of life. But wisdom dictates that you should use strictness whenever decisiveness in matters is needed and use meekness when it is better to use meekness.

In your meekness do not be soft in a way that may

offend you, and in your strictness do not be hard in a way that may offend others.

The Lord Jesus Christ used meekness and used strictness. He was meek and humble of heart and it was said of Him: *"He will not quarrel nor cry out, nor will anyone hear His voice in the streets. A bruised reed He will not break, and a smoking flax He will not quench"* (Matt.12:19,20). The Lord was strict when He upbraided the scribes and the Pharisees severely, saying to them, *"Woe to you, hypocrites!"* (Matt.23). **The Lord Jesus was strict even in rebuking His Apostle Peter.** Once He said to him: *"Get behind Me, Satan! You are an offense to Me, for you are not mindful of the things of God, but the things of men"* (Matt.16:23). To this extent was the Lord Jesus Christ the Meek strict in this situation. In the same way He was strict with Saint Peter when he was embarrassed to let Him wash his feet. He said to him: *"If I do not wash you, you have no part with Me"* (Jn.13:8).

Therefore, there are situations which need strictness, an example of which is the Lord's cleansing of the Temple. Here we see the Lord Jesus Christ the Meek who said to the sinful woman: *"Neither do I condemn you; go and sin no more"* (Jn.8:11) and saved her from the hands of those who were condemning her, driving out the sellers, making a whip of cords, overturning the tables of the moneychangers and ordering the people to take away the doves. **Here in the Lord's strictness we find Him using different degrees of strictness, applying to every condition what suited it.** He overturned the tables of the moneychangers but did not overturn the tables of the doves. He rebuked some by His words and others he drove out, and for others He made a whip of cords. Therefore everything was carried out in discernment according to the need of the situation.

If you prefer meekness and kindness and see someone acting in strictness, do not say: "I have been made to stumble and the ideals have shattered before my eyes". Here appears the danger of focusing on one virtue. The spiritual life is not one virtue, disregarding the others, but it is an integrated life where all the virtues are completed and from all of them one spiritual texture is formed.

In some situations lack of strictness is considered a sin as in the case of Eli the Priest. God punished him severely and took the priesthood from his descendants because he was not strict in bringing up his children. It is true that he drew their attention to their errors, but he did not restrain them and was soft in chastening them (1Sam.3:12-14).

That is why we are not astonished at the strictness with which Saint Peter dealt with Ananias and Sapphira (Acts 5:1-11). He sentenced them to death and did not give them a chance to repent because strictness at that time was necessary for the edification of the Church at its foundation so as to bar any licence, cheating, treason, lying and chaos from entering the Church. That is why it was said after their punishment: *"So great fear came upon all the Church and upon all who heard these things"* (Acts 5:11).

Here we observe an important point: Fear is sometimes as necessary as love, and there is no contradiction in this.

Discerning Between Fear and Love

The Holy Bible says: *"The fear of the Lord is the beginning of wisdom"* (Prov.9:10). Therefore fear from the spiritual point of view is not an error but it is a spiritual stage. He who does not fear God may end in the life of carelessness and indifference, as was said about the unjust judge who *"did not fear God nor regard man"* (Lk.18:2).

In bringing up children, fear is necessary with some of them and in some stages, without which the upbringing fails. The child who does not fear his parents, may walk recklessly with no restraint and become a cause of bitterness for them. Also how easy it is for the student who does not fear his teachers to turn into a disruptive person, wasting the time of his classmates and the nerves of his teachers.

However, we say that fear is a stage that develops and turns into love and reverence. That is why a father or teacher should not blame themselves if they reprimand a son or a student. They should not say in themselves nor in their confession that they have erred because they reprimanded someone and lost their meekness. But on the contrary, their conscience should blame them if they had not been strict at the time when strictness was needed.

Wisdom outlines the limits of reprimanding, that it should spring from a responsible person and in a genuine spiritual way. Saint Paul the Apostle was obliged to upbraid the Galatians who began with the Spirit and tried to be made perfect by the flesh (Gal.3:3). And the sacred zeal sometimes compels a person to be a burning fire. In this case the spiritual aspirant should understand where meekness stands within zealousness. We say that everything under the heavens has its season. Nevertheless, a person can behave zealously without losing his meekness. But it is wrong that a person loses the sacred zeal through his misunderstanding of meekness. We have to understand meekness properly so that we do not think that it is laxity in disposition, or stagnancy.

Some people see Elijah as a model of the sacred zeal and Jeremiah as a model of meekness and tears. But Jeremiah the Prophet was also a model of zeal and of defending the truth. He was not only a man of tears. He who reads the Book of Jeremiah perceives this. David the Prophet was a model of bravery, strength and zeal. And at the same time he was a man of tears, drenching his bed with his tears (Ps.6) and weeping over the death of Absalom and the death of Saul and Jonathan.

The mother who has the wrong compassion for her child which spoils him is not a wise mother and lacks the virtue of discernment. She must know the true meaning of compassion, the extent of compassion, and how far compassion is connected with sound upbringing and with the spiritual and eternal life of her child. The heavenly Father loved His Only Son. Nevertheless, He sacrificed Him for our sake, and on the Cross *"it pleased Him to bruise Him; He has put Him to grief"* as a sin offering for our sake, and *"has laid on Him the iniquity of us all"* (Is.53:1-6). **The discreet physician knows when to use the scalpel, when to use amputation, and when to use pain-killers and tranquillizers.**

The subject of discernment involves the whole spiritual life, and if we talk about it we will talk about all the virtues so what we have mentioned as examples is enough.

The Positive Work and the Inner Work

The Positive Work

Its Importance in Resisting Sin

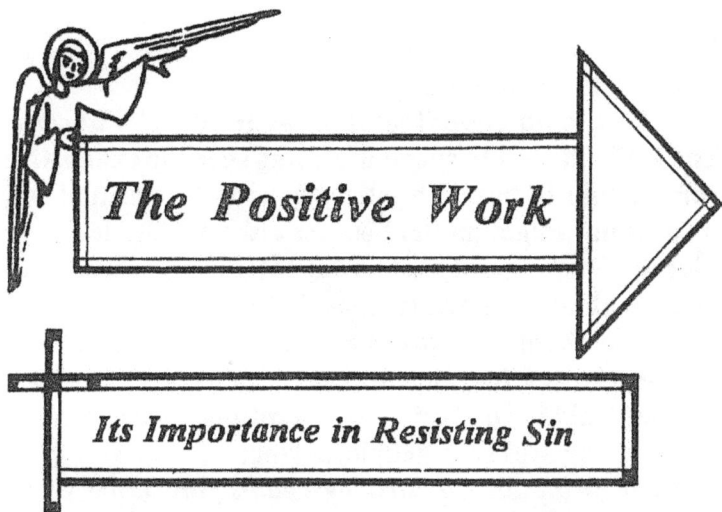

Every person, in edifying his spiritual life, is faced with two important points. One is the resistance of sin in order to cleanse his heart and mind, his senses and his body. This may extend to resisting sin in other people in order to share in purifying the society in which he lives. It is a life of struggle against sin and the devil which represents the passive side of the spiritual life. As for the positive side of the spiritual life, it is edifying the soul and the spirit with virtues, it is life with God, the taste of God and the foretaste of His kingdom. A person tastes the love of God and enjoys His communion in a sacred life.

The person who makes all his life a struggle against sin no doubt suffers much because his life is consumed in combating sin of which the Holy Bible said: *"...she has cast down many wounded, and all who were slain by her were strong men"* (Prov.7:26). And he also consumes his life in struggling with the devil who is a cruel, relentless and evil enemy, and who also, being an expert on the human soul through thousands of years of experience, knows its weaknesses and defects and knows how to bring about its downfall.

There is no doubt that this passive work is irksome and difficult, and to spend life doing so is too exhaustive for the soul to bear. The struggle with the spiritual evil hosts is not a light matter because although the devil lost his sanctity and purity yet he did not lose his nature as an angel with all its potentialities and powers.

What then? Will the person leave the passive side? Will he give up the struggle against sin? No, because this undoubtedly is conducive to submitting to sin, and the Apostle reproves such people, saying: *"You have not yet resisted to bloodshed, striving against sin"* (Heb.12:4). Man should resist the devil, sin and the flesh with all his might and with all the grace which God gives him, and remain steadfast until the last breath of his life.

But the question is: Why is resisting sin difficult? Why did the Lord call it the narrow gate and the difficult path (Matt.7:13,14)? And why did many of the Fathers say that the spiritual life is self-coercion and vanquishing of the self?

It will be thus difficult if it is void of the positive work, if it is mere struggle, *"for the flesh lusts against the Spirit, and the Spirit against the flesh; and these are contrary to one another"* (Gal.5:17). But why this struggle? Because the love for God has not yet entered the heart and has not been established there. How does the love for God enter the heart? It enters through the positive work.

Here appears the importance of the positive work in the spiritual life, without which resistance against sin would be a bitter and difficult task, and may also be unprofitable. We may ask: "Why does the person toil in his spiritual combats? Why does he often fluctuate between failure and success?" Because the love of God is not in his heart, so he struggles out of emptiness. He resists sin and cannot remain steadfast because he does not have the weapons by which he can fight. He does not have the strength by which he can persevere. No doubt the strong weapon by which you overcome sin is your love for God which makes you abhor sin and say: "*How then can I do this great wickedness, and sin against God?*" (Gen.39:9).

If the love for God enters your heart, sin will flee from it completely; sin which causes you to suffer in your struggle against it and makes you inconsistently fall and rise so often.

If the love for God enters your heart you will not fall under the sway of sin and you need not pay great effort in struggling against it. But rather you will not find within yourself this conflict between the flesh and the spirit because you will find yourself by nature alienated to sin. Also the devil will have no place for himself in your heart as the Lord Jesus Christ said: "*...the ruler of this world is coming, and he has nothing in Me*" (Jn:14:30).

You need to struggle against sin because within you

there are worldly lusts which cause you to fall. There are lusts in your heart that resist God. That is why when the devil comes to you, he finds the house decorated, furnished and ready to receive him, so he enters together with his helpers. That is why the desire of the Spirit finds resistance within you from the lusts of the flesh. But if the love of God is in your heart your house will be shielded against sin. And sin will find it in no way easy to attack your heart. Then you will be able to sing with David the Prophet and say to your protected soul: *"Praise the Lord, O Jerusalem! Praise your God, O Zion! For He has strengthened the bars of your gates; He has blessed your children within you"* (Ps.147:12,13).

The love for God within you weakens sin's attacks because there is nothing within you that conforms to it and the doors of your heart become closed before the devil. He cannot penetrate your heart whether by a right blow or a left blow. The love within you shields you. And this love generates within you many children, which are the fruits of the Spirit, the virtues and righteous deeds. That is why the Psalmist does not only say to you that God has strengthened the bars of your gates, which is from the passive side, but he also tells you of the positive side, saying: *"He has blessed your children within you".*

It is a comfortable striving, easy and joyful to the heart. You strive positively for the sake of knowing God and growing in His love. It is completely different from the passive striving in which you struggle against sin and the devil.

The most delightful thing in the spiritual life is this positive act, for it is the taste of God and the foretaste of the Kingdom. It is also to enjoy the life with Him in the depth of His love. Then you will no longer suffer from the spiritual combats nor from the struggle against sin because sin will be incompatible with your nature and rejected by your inner self.

Do you think that man falls into sin because sin is strong, the offenses are severe and the devil's wiles are numerous? No, he falls all the more because his heart is empty of the love for God. If he loves God he will not find sin delicious, nor will he find it difficult to fight against sin but will find himself loathing it because it is extremely wrong and incompatible with his pure nature.

Attaining the Love for God

How can a person attain the love for God? The person attains it through the positive spiritual work which leads him to love God. And his love for God causes him not to err because *"love never fails"* (1Cor.13:8), and as the Apostle Saint Paul said: *"God is love, and he who abides in love abides in God, and God in him"* (1Jn.4:16), and *"he cannot sin, because he has been born of God"* (1Jn.3:9).

Therefore, try to fill your heart with the love of God, then His love inside your heart will be like a burning fire consuming all the lusts of sin together with all its residues and thoughts.

What is the positive work that leads to all this?

Be mindful of God always. Your remembrance of God will generate His love in your heart. His love makes you think more of Him. And each of these leads to and

strengthens the other. If you increase your remembrance of God, of His heaven, of His angels, of His words and commandments, of the eternal bliss with Him, of His beautiful attributes and how He deals with people, then you will be preoccupied with Him. Your preoccupation will make you remember Him more and your remembrance of Him increases your love for Him, and so on.

Your remembrance of God is the first positive work in your spiritual life. God must be before you all the time. You remember Him always, as David said: *"Oh, how I love Your law! It is my meditation all the day"* (Ps.119:97). Your remembrance of God sanctifies your thoughts and generates in your heart spiritual feelings. You will feel timid to think any wrong thought. It will not be easy for you to mingle your sacred thoughts with any abominable thought or even any worldly thought. You will always be encouraged to advance in your Divine thought.

Your remembrance of God leads you to purity of heart because there is no communion whatsoever between light and darkness (2Cor.6:14).

You will become accustomed to prayer. You will also become accustomed to contemplation and ravishment. You will feel you are in God's presence all the time. In this Divine presence the devil will not dare to approach you. If he does he will soon leave you because there is no place for him in you and he will not find you ready for him, seeing that your ways do not agree with his. Even if he fights you with anything it will be a feeble temptation because you are engaged in God. That is why all the devil's combats against you will be concentrated on keeping you away from your preoccupation with God and not in tempting you openly with any sin.

If the devil succeeds in keeping you away from your positive work which is your preoccupation with God then he will proceed to take his next step which is to make you fall into negativeness. Even in this condition, having acquired strength from your previous spiritual act, you will be able to resist his temptations. **In this case he will tempt you whilst respecting and fearing you, taking his guard against you and therefore will not attack you severely with all his might.** But the person who is far from the positive work is an easy prey for the devils. They do not fear him because they know that he is without any strength from within that can fight them.

Reading is very beneficial as a positive work that absorbs the intellect in God. It provides the person with matter for contemplation and prayer. It reminds me of the raising of incense which prepares the altar for the oblations to be offered. Reading brings your thoughts into a spiritual atmosphere and brings to your remembrance God and His saints. The word of God is efficacious. It works in you and gives fervour to your spirituality and prompts you with ardour to the Lord's path. It enlightens your thoughts and generates in you spiritual feelings, and strengthens your will to walk in God's path.

Similarly, spiritual gatherings are beneficial for uniting the person with God because they involve prayers, readings, hymns and spiritual songs and beneficial sayings. All these bring you into a spiritual atmosphere from which the devil feels estranged.

Spiritual friendship is very beneficial. It is one of the positive works which strengthens your heart and attracts you towards God. Your spiritual friend is the one whom whenever you see you mention God and His commandments, convict yourself of your sins, and from whom you learn the life of virtue. Sin could not enter the life of Lot and his family when they were living with our father Abraham. But it found a chance when they were away from this spiritual friendship living in Sodom where Lot tormented himself with the errors of its inhabitants.

Partaking of the Sacrament of the Eucharist is one of the most important positive works with all its deep efficacies on the soul and all that it entails of continual repentance and confession. The Lord Jesus Christ said of the person who partakes of the Holy Communion that he *"abides in Me and I in him"* (Jn.6:56). And we say in the Holy Liturgy: "We partake of Your Holy Mysteries for the sanctification of our souls, bodies and spirits".

What have you acquired of these spiritual works? And what have you learnt of the spiritual practices by which you train yourself on the life of the Spirit and the fruit of the Spirit, which engage your daily thoughts in your eternity and its necessary deeds? How far do you observe giving an account of yourself and of convicting yourself of all your inadequacies and errors? How far do you keep your prostrations, fasts, and conduct in the life of the Spirit?

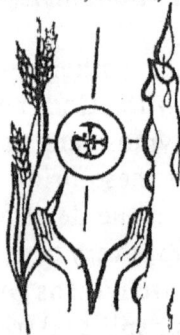

Benefits of the Positive Work

Through all these positive works you set up within yourself a balance between the impact of the world and that of the Spirit. If the devil approaches you to tempt you and finds you with no Bible or psalm, no prayer or contemplation, no spiritual meditation or spiritual gathering, with no fasts or prostrations, with neither confession nor Holy Communion, what state will you be in? And how will you be able to resist sin without any weapon? You will then be like a city attacked by the enemy and a city which has neither army nor weapons nor fortifications.

Take this rule and set it before you: Every person who falls into sin must have been away from the positive work for a long time, whether it be the spiritual means of grace or the practice of virtue or the love of God. Thus sin comes to a person when he is unprepared for it, or it comes to him when he is in a state of weakness or listlessness. Listen to what our Lord says: *"And pray that your flight may not be in winter or on the Sabbath"* (Matt.24:20). *In winter* means in the time of spiritual coolness. *On the Sabbath* means during the time when you do not do any work. Both matters remind us of the abandoning of the positive spiritual work. Therefore, always be alert in your heart. Let there be oil in your lamp. And as the Lord said about this readiness: *"Let your waist be girded and your lamps burning"* (Lk.12:35).

Concern yourself with the spiritual work which grants you strength to resist sin. Fill your stores with spiritual practices so that you may not be overcome by the years of scantiness with its famine and deficiency. Keep your stone in your sling, so that if Goliath appears before you, you may be able to go forward and say with trust: *"This day the Lord will deliver you into my hand"* (1Sam.17:46). And do not limit your striving to only resisting the negatives because this is exhaustive, but also strive in the positive work which gives you the strength by which you fight sin. May the Lord be with you.

The Inner Work

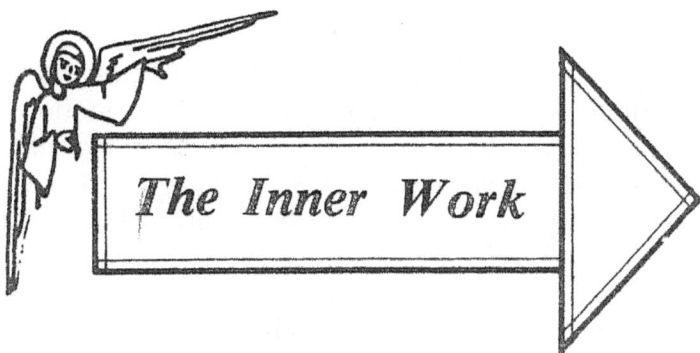

The Importance of the Inner Work

The spiritual life is not just outward practices performed by the body. But its spiritual criterion depends on the person's spiritual state from within, with regard to his intentions and impulses, the feelings of his heart and the state of his mind. We should not forget the saying of the Lord in this respect: *"My son, give Me your heart"* (Prov.23:26), and His saying: *"Keep your heart with all diligence, for out of it springs the issues of life"* (Prov.4:23).

This means that virtues start in the heart. Then they spring from the heart and are manifest in the person's deeds. Every good external deed which does not spring from the heart is by no means counted as a virtue. The Lord rejected every worship offered to Him that did not come from a pure heart. He said, reprimanding the Jews: *"This people honours Me with their lips, but their heart is far from Me"* (Mk.7:6).

Therefore it is not fitting to be concerned with the external appearance of virtues nor to be sufficed with

them. We give you an example.

When a person wants to abandon anger, he trains himself to quieten his countenance and his motions. Thus he abandons the loud and harsh voice and appears to be calm with quiet nerves, free from any excitement. But all this quietness is from without only and his heart from within is a fiery furnace, full of suppressed anger. Of course it is good that you should not rage so that you do not err with your tongue and lose your relationship with others. But undoubtedly the external quietness is by no means sufficient and there should be an inner work which quietens the heart also. The quietness of the heart is achieved through training it on forbearance and meekness, on love for others and on blaming oneself. Thus you convince yourself from within so that your heart will not move wrongly even though it is not apparent to others. This reminds us of what the Fathers said about the meaning of turning the other cheek.

What is the meaning of: *"But whoever slaps you on the right cheek, turn the other to him also"* (Matt.5:39)? Some of the Fathers said, as written in the book of John Cassian: "The first slap is from the outside, on the cheek, that is, an external insult. This is met by turning the other cheek which is the inner slap by referring the blame to oneself". You say to yourself, "I deserve all this because of my sins". So the second slap you take is from your heart from within.

This symbolic meaning of the commandment of turning the other cheek conforms with David's behaviour when he was insulted by Shimei the son of Gera. When the commander of the army wanted to kill him, David prevented him saying: *"So let him curse, because the Lord has said to him, 'Curse David'... It may be that the Lord will look on my affliction"* (2Sam.16:5-12).

This also conforms with the saying of Saint Abba Antony the Great: "If someone reproaches you from without, reprove yourself from within", that there may be a balance within and without you and thus you will not suffer. Some people forbear outwardly in a seemingly quiet way while they suffer inwardly, feeling injustice. Thus there is conflict between the inside and the outside. But through the inner spiritual work the person is saved from this contradiction either by humility, that is, by blaming oneself and remembering one's own sins or by joyfulness, that is, by entering into the fellowship of God's sufferings (Phil.3:10). Thus the person rejoices in suffering like the Apostles who, after they were beaten, *"departed from the presence of the council, rejoicing that they were counted worthy to suffer shame for His name"* (Acts 5:41).

The Inner Work in Repentance

As an external work, repentance is abandoning sin and keeping away from it and from its causes. Yet a person might leave sin while in his heart there remains a desire towards it. Can we call this repentance? No, because there should be an inner work within the heart until the person reaches the point of detesting sin. And this is the true repentance, when a person puts in his heart the desire to live with God instead of the lust of the material and the flesh.

Here we would like to explain the true spiritual meaning of a metanoia or prostration. In the metanoia the person makes a prostration, he bows down and his head touches the ground, that is, the dust. This is the external apparent work. But there is an inner work which should accompany the bowing down of the body. The person should bow down his soul from within in contrition so as to abandon its haughtiness, as David the Prophet said: *"My soul clings to the dust"* (Ps.119:25). Someone said to one of the Fathers: "Sometimes I make a metanoia before my brother apologizing to him but he does not accept it".

The Father answered: "It is because you did it in haughtiness". This means that the body bowed down whilst the soul remained in its haughtiness and did not reach the dust.

Therefore repentance, whether in reconciling with God or with our fellow men, is an inner work of totally convincing the soul of the way of repentance and of the person's desire to repent, and of the need of the soul to feel remorse for its past life. All these works are carried out from within. The matter is not just abandoning the offenses from the outside because even if all things that offend encompass us externally, they cannot harm us so long as the heart from within prevails. Saint John Chrysostom rightly said: "No one can harm a person unless the person harms himself".

The Inner Work in Upbringing and in the Ministry

Preachers often stand at the pulpit and renounce the indecent apparel of young girls, the long hair of young men, and the like. All these are external matters which youth may give up when under pressure, but their hearts remain uncleaned. The solution is the inner work, by bringing the love of God and the love of sanctity into the hearts of these people, convincing them that the beauty of the soul is far more important than the beauty of the body. Then they will abandon their present state willingly and contently. They will start to love the decent life and walk in it with seriousness, not for the sake of obedience nor out of fear, but out of purity of heart. Then they will need no supervisor nor blaming and will not enter into any conflict. This is the true upbringing which depends on the inner work of convincing and cultivating high principles in the soul.

Therefore instruct the inward parts of your children and not their outward parts. Work with your spirituality inside their hearts. Before you use the rod from the outside cultivate in them the love of God first. And trust that the love of God is far mightier than the rod and that it can peacefully repel every sin from the heart. As the Lord Jesus Christ commanded, cleanse first the inside of the cup and dish, so that their outside may be clean also (Matt.23:26).

The aim of the inner work is first to prevail over the self, and then to attain purity of soul. This needs

convincing the soul in a sound way. In order for the soul
to be convinced there should be a true understanding of
matters, of the meaning of life and its goal, the meaning
of freedom and its boundaries, the meaning of strength,
the meaning of beauty, the meaning of manliness, and
also the true concept of religion and the manner of
dealing with people.

In instructing people, we do not use the rod, but we
use convincing and sound understanding. Then
afterwards comes strengthening their will which is an
inner work in the heart and mind. How easy is the
chastisement of the outside of man. But is this
upbringing? No, it is not. Even if this way brings about
some results, in most cases they are temporary and
vanish after a while with the vanishing of the external
pressures. Does the person who yields to these pressures
have any reward from God? What sort of reward when
he walks in virtue only externally, and unwillingly?
Therefore the inner work has two parts: our work within
ourselves and our work within other people.

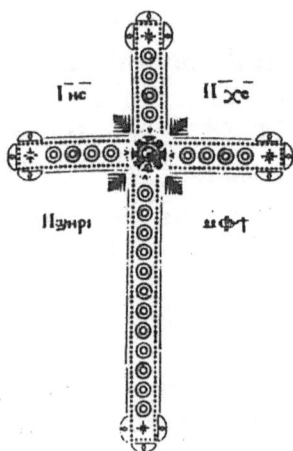

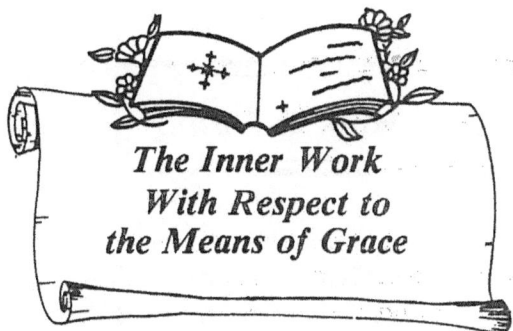

The Inner Work in Prayer

Is prayer merely talking with God? Or is there an inner work? What is this inner work? Talking with God is the obvious external work in prayer, but undoubtedly there are more important inner works, which are the feeling of the soul's contact with God and of being near Him, and the accompanying feelings of love, awe, faith, ardour, and rapture of being in His presence. Or rather, prayer sometimes reaches beyond the limits of talking with God, as the spiritual elder said: **"Silence your tongue that your heart may speak, and silence your heart that God may speak"**. This is the inner work in prayer which is first of all the encounter of man with God and secondly listening to the voice of God within the soul, or at least the deep spiritual feeling of the Divine presence. Have you reached this level? Or are you sufficed with the external work? Here we see that part of the inner work is from you and part reaches you as a gift from God Himself.

The Inner Work in Fasting

Many people confine themselves in their fasts to the external work which is abstaining from food for a certain period of time and then limiting what they eat to the unappetizing. But the inner work which is neglected by such people is that of preventing the soul from any wrong desire and preventing the flesh from eating desirous food, using the period of fasting to raise the spirit above the level of the flesh, giving her concentrated spiritual nourishment which lasts even after the period of fasting. Is it so with you? Or do you suffice yourself with the external bodily work and think that you fast?

The Inner Work in Reading

Reading is an external work, but contemplation on what you read is an inner work. That is why contemplation is more important than reading. Understanding is an inner work, and so is the effect of the words on you and the carrying out of what you read. Therefore the inner work in reading means the spiritual work and not just the knowledge by which you add information to your mind. The inner work in reading is the transformation of the words into life.

The Inner Work in Keeping Silence

Abstaining from speech is the external appearance of silence. But silence is not confined to the negative side only. It has its positive sides as well.

The inner work of silence is that the person delves into his inner self to gain spiritual benefits, contemplate, think on the Divine attributes, and pray. Thus he benefits spiritually from his silence. He does not talk with people because at the same time he is talking with God. That is why he sits alone to enjoy God. **Solitude is not just sitting by oneself** because what is the virtue in a person's sitting alone? He may sit alone while his thoughts wander here and there. Sitting alone is just an external work, the aim of which is to sit with God or to be alone with Him and enjoy His Divine communion in prayer, contemplation, praise, confession and love. This is the inner work in solitude.

We ought to give attention to the inner work with all our might because the Holy Bible says that *"the kingdom of God is inside you"* (Lk.17:21). If, through the inner work, we reach the kingdom of God within us, then we will have reached the profound spiritual work in which God reigns over the heart, the thought, the feeling and emotions and the whole of our being. Every worship which does not bring us to this aim must have strayed from the path.

The inner work has two sides, the work with God and the work with the soul. You work with your soul so as to control it well and observe its thoughts, feelings and desires and reprove it when it deviates and return it to the right way and convince it of the way of the Lord and its beauty, reminding it of eternal life so that it prepares itself for it diligently with all seriousness and striving. **Your work with God is to wrestle with Him so that He affirms His kingdom, and to converse with Him with affectionate love.**

To have a relationship with God and deepen it day by day is undoubtedly an inner work, which is incompatible with external semblance. Spiritual life is not merely external practices, laws and statutes, but it is love for God and men. And love is an inner work that needs vigilance, preservation and growth. This is with regard to the people who live in the world. As for the monks their inner work is higher and deeper. This leads us to ask: **What is the meaning of a working monk?**

The working monk is the one who is continually preoccupied with the inner work so that his mind and thoughts are unceasingly engaged in God. If it was said about monasticism that it is the detachment from all to be attached to the One, therefore the inner work of the monk is how to attach his mind unceasingly to God and how to bind his emotions with the love of God, repelling every other thought. That is why he has to engage himself in prayer, contemplation, praise, singing and spiritual reading so that his mind can always be with God. Because if he does not do this his mind will wander and fall into frivolity.

The monk's inner work with God compels him by necessity to keep silence, as Saint Arsenius said: "I cannot talk with God and people at the same time", and as one of the monk fathers said: "The talkative person reveals that he is void from within", that is, void of the inner work. That is why the Fathers chose solitude and were circumspect on keeping silence and preserving the senses so as to continue in their inner work with God until they attained unceasing prayer and crucifying the mind to avoid falling into frivolity.

Benefits of the Inner Work

The foremost benefit of the inner work is the perpetual abiding in God. And the more the person clings to God, the more humble he becomes because he feels his weakness in his inability to detach himself from all to be attached to the One. **The devil does not leave this inner work without attack or hindrance.** He tries with all his might to disperse the person's thoughts, presenting tens of subjects and giving the person the feeling of their urgency so as to preoccupy him with them. He may send the person visitors or friends to stop him from his spiritual work, as well as countless matters. He may attack the pastor with the preoccupations of his pastorate to absorb his time and attention away from being alone with God.

CHAPTER EIGHT

Faithfulness

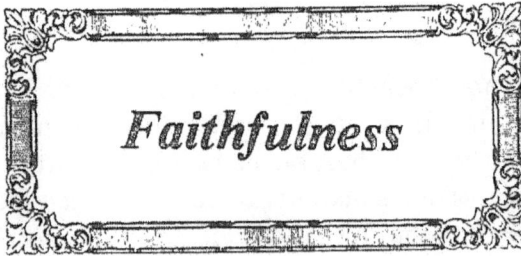

The Importance and Extent of Faithfulness

By faithfulness, I do not merely mean honesty in monetary and material matters, in which a person does not rob or plunder others, but I mean faithfulness in its full sense, that is, faithfulness in the whole of one's behaviour and spiritual life: **faithfulness in man's relationship with God, with others and with himself.**

The Lord Jesus Christ called us to this faithfulness when He talked about the faithfulness in the ministry and about the prudent and faithful steward *"whom his master will make ruler over his household, to give them their portion of food in due season"* (Lk.12:42). Moreover **the Lord Jesus Christ also mentioned that faithfulness is the criterion of Judgment and the basis of entry into the Kingdom.** For He will say to the person who merits entry into His kingdom: *"Well done, good and faithful servant; you were faithful over a few things, I will make you ruler over many things. Enter into the joy of your Lord"* (Matt.25:21,23).

But to what extent should we be faithful? The Lord says: *"Be faithful until death, and I will give you the crown of life"* (Rev.2:10). *"Until death"*, that is, to the point at which you sacrifice your self and expend your life for the sake of faithfulness. This reminds us of the words of Saint Paul the Apostle to the Hebrews when he upbraided them for their faithlessness in resisting sin, saying: *"You have not yet resisted to bloodshed, striving against sin"* (Heb.12:4). *"Until death"*, that is, even if the matter leads to shedding one's blood in striving against sin. Thus the person is faithful in his relationship with God, not betraying Him by yielding to sin.

Faithfulness helped the righteous attain their goal. Many simultaneously started the path but some attained while others did not and yet others tarried. What was the reason for this difference? It was because some - contrary to others - were faithful in all their devotional practices and thus were able to gain crowns.

Faithfulness should be in worldly matters as well as in spiritual matters. In the same way as the person gives concern to his spiritual life, he should also be faithful in every work he does. The student should be faithful in his studies and the labourer in perfecting his work and keeping his time, likewise with the employee and whoever is in responsibility.

The chaste Joseph was a spiritual person and honest in his work. He was so honest in his service to Potiphar that his work prospered. He was so sincere in his work as a minister for Egypt that he saved it and the surrounding countries from famine. He was so honest in his work when he was a prisoner that the jailer entrusted him with responsibilities.

In practical life there are matters which test a

person's honesty. An example is when a person obtains a false sick certificate to get undeserved leave from work. It does not suffice him to be dishonest himself but he makes the doctor err as well. Another example is when a person claims overtime allowance or reimbursements when he could have performed the work during normal working hours. **The examples are numerous,** among them are those who spread news dishonestly, those who disclose secrets entrusted to them and those who do not perfect the errands given to them.

Your Faithfulness to God

If God is so faithful to us to the extent of Incarnation and Redemption, and if His love and His sacrifice have reached such an extent, how much more should we be faithful?

Your faithfulness towards God means that you do not betray Him at all. An analogy to illustrate this is the wife who is faithful to her husband. No matter how much freedom and trust he gives her, she is faithful to him and does not betray him nor does she have a relationship with another. Likewise your soul, which is the bride of Christ, should not betray Him with worldliness or with Satan, or with any lust or evil thought.

Your heart which belongs to God should not be opened to His enemies. The faithful person should not be lenient towards any sin because sin is enmity with God, nor should he entertain any erring thought but with all faithfulness he should repel it immediately. He should never accept any matter that would sever his cleaving to God, considering that every sin is foremost directed against God because it is against His love and incompatible with His will. It is against His commandments and against abiding in Him. He should emulate Joseph who transcended sin, saying: *"How then can I do this great wickedness, and sin against God?"* (Gen.39:9). Joseph considered that sin was not chiefly directed against Potiphar or his wife but against God. For the same reason David the Prophet said to the Lord in Psalm 51: *"Against You, You only, have I sinned and done this evil in Your sight"* (Ps.51:4).

Sin is separation from God and a rebellion against Him. The faithful person in his relationship with God never accepts anything that would sever him from God, as Saint Paul the Apostle said, *"For I am persuaded that neither death nor life, nor angels nor principalities nor powers, nor things present nor things to come, nor height nor depth, nor any other created thing, shall be able to separate us from the love of God which is in Christ Jesus our Lord"* (Rom.8:38,39).

Those who in truth knew God never abandoned Him. As examples, we present to you the Saints of Repentance. When they repented and tasted the love of God they did not return to sin which would have severed them from the love of God. But they continued in their growth in love until they reached high levels of perfection. We mention Saint Augustine, Saint Moses the Black, Saint Mary of Egypt and Saint Pelagia. About his erstwhile life of sin, Saint Augustine said to God: "I **have tarried long in loving You, O Inexpressible Beauty**", acknowledging and considering that whilst in sin he was alienated from the love of God.

This is from the negative side, but from the positive side faithfulness to God necessitates that a person be faithful in all his spiritual practices: in his prayers because they are conversing with God, in his reading of the Holy Bible through which he listens to the voice of God, in his contemplation and in his praise, in his confessions, in his partaking of the Holy Communion and in his fasts.

The pastor also should be faithful in his ministry and in his spiritual activities. He should be faithful in teaching, as the Apostle said: *"But as for you, speak the things which are proper for sound doctrine"* (Titus 2:1). He should not present his own opinions as dogmas and should not present to people except the teachings which he received from the Church through her saints as Saint Paul said to his disciple Timothy: *"And the things that you have heard from me among many witnesses, commit these to faithful men who will be able to teach others also"* (2Tim.2:2). **As he should be faithful in teaching he should also be faithful in visitation and in bringing back the stray.** The Lord Jesus gave us examples of this in His looking for the lost sheep (Lk.15), in His work for the sake of Zacchaeus and the sinful woman, and in saying that He came *"to serve and to give his life a ransom for many"* (Mk.10:45).

With regard to faithfulness in the ministry we quote the words of the Holy Bible: *"Cursed is he who does the work of the Lord deceitfully"* (Jer.48:10). He who is faithful in the work of the Lord acts with all ardour, diligently, sincerely, with sacred zeal and with all love and heartfelt feeling. He toils for the sake of the Lord. He does not give sleep to his eyes nor slumber to his eyelids until he finds a place for the Lord in every heart, as is written in the Didache about the bishop, that he should care for the salvation of all. And these words apply to all the bishops' assistants.

Such was the faithfulness in the ministry which our fathers the Apostles lived. They witnessed to the Lord with all sincerity. They were faithful witnesses, spreading the message to all the countries of the world as the Psalm says of them, that their words went out to the end of the world (Ps.19). They did that work boldly with all their might, enduring imprisonment, scourging, persecution and torture, saying their famous declaration: *"We ought to obey God rather than men"* (Acts 5:29). As an example of this faithfulness Saint Paul the Apostle said: *"I have fought the good fight, I have finished the race, I have kept the faith",* (2Tim.4:7) *"And I thank Christ Jesus our Lord who has enabled me, because He counted me faithful, putting me into the ministry"* (1Tim.1:12). That is why Saint Paul praised those who helped him for their faithfulness in the ministry, saying: *"Tychicus, a beloved brother and faithful minister in the Lord"* (Eph.6:21), *"Epaphras, our dear fellow servant, who is a faithful minister of Christ"* (Col.1:7), *"Onesimus, a faithful and beloved brother"* (Col.4:9), and *"Timothy, who is my beloved and faithful son in the Lord"* (1Cor.4:17).

For this reason it is said about the minister that he is entrusted with the ministry, or that God entrusted him with the ministry. To this effect, Saint Paul the Apostle says: *"...preaching which was committed to me",* (Titus 1:3) *"the gospel for the uncircumcised had been committed to me",* (Gal.2:7) and: *"I have been entrusted with a stewardship... woe is me if I do not preach the*

Gospel" (1Cor.9:17,16). Therefore the ministry is a commitment before God in which the minister should be faithful, and it is not a mere title.

He who is faithful in his relationship with God is also faithful in his promises and vows, from the first promise uttered by his godparent in renouncing Satan on his behalf on the day of his baptism to all the promises which he is or is not mindful of, including the promises he makes every time he partakes of the Holy Communion, and his promises on all occasions especially in times of affliction. Into this realm comes vows of which the Holy Bible says: *"It is better not to vow than to vow and not pay"* (Ecc.5:5). That is why you have to sit alone with yourself and recall all your promises and vows in order to pay them - even though late it is better than complete negligence. Do not try after vowing to return and discuss the matter anew, negotiate and try to change and replace or get rid of your vow and your promise. Before vowing or promising, the Holy Bible enjoins you, saying: *"Do not be rash with your mouth, and let not your heart utter anything hastily before God"* (Ecc.5:2).

Your faithfulness to God also comprises your honesty in paying the tithes and firstfruits. They are not yours but they are God's portion. You pay them to those who ought to have them, to the church or to the poor, otherwise the money would be 'unlawful' to you. You would have kept it with you and been unjust to those who ought to have it. About this money and the like the Holy Bible says: *"...make friends for yourselves by unrighteous mammon"* (Lk.16:9). And thus says the Lord God in the Book of Malachi the Prophet: *"Will a man rob God? Yet you have robbed Me! But you say, 'In what way have we robbed You?' In tithes and offerings"* (Mal.3:8).

Your Faithfulness to Yourself

This constitutes many elements: Your faithfulness over your eternity, your concern about your spirit and your spiritual growth, your sincerity in resisting sin and your honesty with your time and intellect.

He who is faithful over his eternity exerts every effort to attain to it. He considers himself a sojourner on earth, lusting for nothing therein. All his desires are focused on eternity as the Holy Bible says: *"...we do not look at the things which are seen, but at the things which are not seen. For the things which are seen are temporary, but the things which are not seen are eternal"* (2Cor.4:18).

Therefore, such a person pays more attention to his spirit than to his body, contrary to what we notice in our everyday life. For many care for their body, for its food, clothing, health, strength and treatment whilst they do not care at all for their souls as though the thought of their eternity had never crossed their minds.

Those who are faithful over their eternity care for their spiritual nourishment. They provide their spirit with all her needs of the word of God and contemplation, prayer and spiritual songs, spiritual gatherings and friendships. They provide her with the nourishment of the Eucharist, the love of God, the fruit of the Spirit and beneficial spiritual practices. Is it so with you?

Those who are faithful over their eternity give attention to the health of their spirit. If they see any spiritual illness creeping into them, they recourse to the

Physician of our bodies and souls, our God who gives strength through His Holy Spirit. They also consult the spiritual fathers and counsellors seeking healing for their souls from every sinful desire and evil thought.

Those who are faithful over their spirit always give attention to their spiritual growth. They are never sufficed with any spiritual level they attain because God asks them to be perfect and to be saints, saying: *"Therefore you shall be perfect, just as your Father in heaven is perfect"* (Matt.5:48), and also the Holy Bible says: *"...but as He who called you is holy, you also be holy in all your conduct"* (1Pet.1:15).

That is why those who are faithful over their spirits live in hunger and thirst for righteousness. They gain the blessedness of which the Lord promised in the Gospel of Saint Matthew (Matt.5:6). Their thirst for the Lord does not end. The more they drink the more they ask, saying with David the Prophet, the Psalmist and man of prayer, *"My soul thirsts for You; My flesh longs for You in a dry and thirsty land where there is no water. As the deer pants for the water brooks, so pants my soul for You, O God"* (Ps.63:1,42:1). No matter how high they reach in virtue they still feel their need for more, like Saint Paul the Apostle who, although he was caught up to the third heaven (2Cor.12:2,4), said: *"Not that I have already attained, or am already perfected; but I press on, that I may lay hold of that for which Christ Jesus has also laid hold of me. I do not count myself to have apprehended; but one thing I do, forgetting those things which are behind and reaching forward to those things which are ahead. I press towards the goal for the prize of the upward call of God in Christ Jesus"* (Phil.3:12-14).

Thus he who is faithful in his spirituality lives in

continual growth. He is like the tree which grows everyday whether you notice its growth or not. Regarding this the Psalm says: *"The righteous shall flourish like a palm tree, he shall grow like a cedar in Lebanon"* (Ps.92:12). He advances in his prayer, in depth and in length. He advances in his faith, in his humility and in his love. He also advances in giving and expending. He does not stop at a certain point but blames himself whenever he ceases to grow.

In his growth, he does not only seek his eternity but also his place there. As long as everyone will receive his reward according to his labour (1Cor.3:8), so he toils with all his might to receive a greater reward. As long as *"one star differs from another star in glory"* (1Cor.15:41), so he labours to deserve all the heavenly glory, striving in his love for God and growing in this love continually so that he can enjoy these promises in eternity, feeling that his growth in the love for God not only helps him to attain a more gleeful eternal life but that it also protects him here from falling, and faithfulness calls him to advance.

Is it so with you? Do you grow everyday? Or are you standing still and has your growth ceased? Or have you deteriorated and has your former love turned lukewarm? Or do you still need to repent in order to rise? Ask yourself. If it is so with you, then faithfulness necessitates your vigorous striving to resist sin.

Be on your guard not to leave any of the doors of your soul open to sin. With all faithfulness close all the openings through which Satan can enter. Be faithful in controlling your intellect and senses because the senses are the doors to the intellect, and the intellect is a door through which lusts enter into the heart. As for you, sing with David the Prophet and say: *"Praise the Lord, O Jerusalem! Praise your God, O Zion! For He has strengthened the bars of your gates; and has blessed your children within you"* (Ps.147:12). How true is what is said in the Song of Songs: *"A garden enclosed is my sister, my spouse, a spring shut up, a fountain sealed"* (Song 4:12). It is a garden full of the fruits of the Holy Spirit but it is shut before the enemy and all his thoughts and all his wiles. He cannot enter because the Lord is within. It is a temple of His Holy Spirit (1Cor.3:16). Therefore it is firmly shielded against the attacks of the enemy.

Such a faithful soul is like a ship without any holes. There is not one single hole through which water can enter. It is surrounded with water on all sides, yet only from the outside. The water cannot find an opening through which it can penetrate. Such is the faithful person. If he finds the devil trying to drill holes for himself in his soul, he hastens without slothfulness to cure it and his soul remains sound. The devil fights his soul from the outside but is unable to enter.

He who is faithful in his spirituality does not justify himself if he falls. He does not give the excuse of his weakness or the severity of the warfare that encountered him, but he resists even to death. The chaste Joseph refused to sin, giving not the excuse of his pressing circumstances. Also Daniel the Prophet and the three saintly youths cleaved to the Lord, presenting not the excuse of their being prisoners in exile and that the threats, the lions' den and the fiery furnace, were severe and fearful, but they persevered and remained steadfast. Such were the martyrs before the various sorts of tortures and terrors.

The faithful person is a steadfast person, fighting the Lord's battle valiantly. He does not say that anything happened against his will. He withstands the toughest spiritual war in the same way as David did before Goliath the giant: with all faith and with no fear, trusting that God would give him the victory.

He who is faithful in his warfare is mindful of what is said of the valiant soldier, that **he fights to the last bullet and to the last man.** In other words, with all his effort and with all the help and grace he is given. He does not yield at all to the enemy nor betray the Lord nor depend on presenting certain excuses. The Holy Bible and Tradition are full of examples of such strong and faithful individuals who persisted in the love of God despite the circumstances they were in.

If there is faithfulness of heart there will be faithfulness of will. He who wills is capable. If he lacks strength he will ask for it from above and it will reach him. That is why in Saint Peter the Apostle's discourse about the power of the devil and how he is like a roaring lion, seeking whom he may devour, we find him saying afterwards: *"Resist him, steadfast in the faith"* (1Pet.5:9). Yes, resistance denotes faithfulness, provided that it is a serious resistance from the depth of the heart and constituting the whole of one's will.

What will the result of resistance be? Saint James the Apostle says: *"Resist the devil and he will flee from you"* (Jas.4:7). Therefore, the importance lies in the pure and faithful heart which wills to resist and prompts the will to resist. That is why the Lord, before healing the paralysed man at Bethesda, enquired about the state of the man's heart, asking him, *"Do you want to be made well?"*

One of the devil's practices is that he feels your pulse

first: Would you give way to him even in the very smallest matter? If you would he dares to move to a greater matter. If you open before him a little hole, even the size of a needle's eye, he will attack you more violently because there and then he realizes that your faithfulness to God is not perfect. If you give way in the small matters, he is encouraged to find in you a place for himself or a weak spot to use.

If you are lax in controlling the senses, he will attack you in the intellect.

If you are lax in the intellect, he will fight you with lust.

And if you are lax in lust he will fight you to accomplish the deed.

Therefore do not be lax in anything at all. If you fall in one step hasten and rise and do not advance to another. Faithfulness necessitates that you watch over your soul and not be negligent of its purity and its salvation. If you find the devil throwing something evil into your thoughts quickly remember the words of the Holy Bible: *"Bringing every thought into captivity to the obedience of Christ"* (2Cor.10:5).

He who is faithful over his eternity and spirituality is watchful over his soul. He does not wait until he falls into a fatal lapse but if he finds listlessness creeping into his soul he hastens to cure it before it develops. He resists sin at its onset and does not wait until it reaches the point of seriousness that would afflict him. This is because if he is slack in resisting the devil, the devil will not be tolerant with him.

He who is faithful does not use his weak potentials as pretexts, but he tries continually to develop them. He also does not present his incapability as an excuse because God is capable of granting him strength. And God is faithful who does not permit anyone to be tempted beyond his capability. Thus says the Apostle: *"But God is faithful, who will not allow you to be tempted beyond what you are able, but with the temptation will also make the way of escape, that you may be able to bear it"* (1Cor.10:13).

The spiritual person is honest regarding time. He uses it in whatever is beneficial to him in every respect; spiritually, intellectually and in serving others. He sees that time is part of his life, a talent entrusted to him, which he should not waste but spend in doing good. Therefore, look how much of your time you have wasted in vain and ask yourself: "Am I faithful regarding my time"?

Consider your faithfulness on the Day of the Lord. It is the Lord's Day. It belongs to Him. If you are not faithful in spending this Day in a spiritual way then you are not faithful to the Lord nor to yourself. What is said about Sunday as the Day of the Lord is also said about the feasts of the Lord. They are the Lord's. They belong to Him. They are holy days. The Lord says in the Book of Leviticus: *"The feasts of the Lord, which you shall proclaim to be holy convocations, these are My feasts"* (Lev.23:2). And the Lord mentioned that His feasts are as holy as the Sabbath (Lev.23:8,25,32,39). **Are you faithful on the Days of the Lord and on His feasts? Do you keep them holy?**

Your Faithfulness to Others

The faithful person, inasmuch as he is faithful over the kingdom of God within himself, is also faithful over the kingdom of God within others. He loves others as himself. He cares for them as he cares for himself. He is concerned about their salvation, their growth and their felicity as much as he cares for himself. For such is the commandment (Matt.22:39).

When God created the fruit tree, He did not create it barren but He put in it an important quality which made it *"yield fruit according to its kind, whose seed is in itself"* (Gen.1:11). And He also created the herb to yield seed according to its kind. Are you similar to these trees? Do you bring forth fruit of your kind, and does your seed yield fruit of its kind as well? Do you spread the Kingdom of heaven wherever you go? How far are you faithful to the kingdom of God?

I shall ask you some questions. Reply to them to yourself and also before your father confessor:

If you enter a house, does the word of God enter with you? If you live among people, friends, acquaintances or collegues, do you bear in them spiritual fruit whether by word or by good example or by both? If you visit people, do they say in their hearts: "Today Christ visited us"? Does the blessing of God reach people through you?

Do you become in your faithfulness, salt for the earth and light for the world? Is this not the Lord's commandment in His Sermon on the Mount

172

(Matt.5:13,14)? Are we faithful in keeping this commandment? Saint Peter the Apostle says: *"...receiving the end of your faith- the salvation of your souls"* (1Pet.1:9), and Saint Paul the Apostle says: *"I have become all things to all men, that I might by all means save some"* (1Cor.9:22), and moreover he says: *"I have made myself a servant to all, that I might win the more"* (1Cor.9:19). And Saint Ignatius of Antioch was surnamed 'Theophorus' which means 'bearer of God'. **Are you also a Theophorus, bearing God** to all so that everyone sees Him in your life? Do you build His kingdom in all your relationships?

Faithfulness in the Few Things

How Can I Be Faithful?

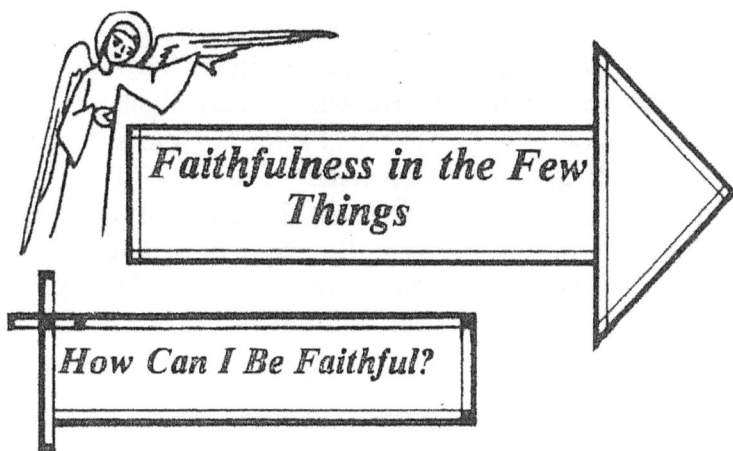

Someone may ask: "The spiritual path is long. How can I reach its end? How can I reach the sanctity without which no one will see God? How can I reach the perfection that is required of me?" The reply is easy and feasible: **Be faithful in the the few things and God will entrust you with much.** For this is God's way and this is His promise, and this is what He will say to people in the Day of Judgment (Matt.25:21,23). Therefore, this is all that you have to do. You do not have to think of getting to the destination in one go. But you should know that one single step is the beginning of the longest journey.

Be faithful in the first step then God will entrust you with the rest. Be faithful in your spiritual goal then God will design for you the means to reach the goal. Be faithful in the intention and God will entrust you with the deed.

The devil may complicate the way and make it appear difficult before you, instilling within you fears which make you imagine that there are too many things requested of you which are not in your power and beyond your capabilities, to make you despair. But God requests from you only faithfulness in the few things. As for the many things, He will entrust them to you. Therefore it is beautiful that Psalm 119 starts with the verse: *"Blessed are the blameless in the way"* (Ps.119:1). It suffices that you walk in the path of the Lord blamelessly. That is what He requires of you. As for reaching the destination, leave it to Him. He disposes with His own hand when and how.

Ministry and Dedication

Someone may ask: "How can my whole life be for the Lord? Is it possible that God would grant me to devote my life to Him? Is it possible that all my life can be for His service? How?". I say to you:

Start with the little you are capable of, by giving your spare time to the Lord. Start by consecrating the Day of the Lord. If you are faithful in this God may entrust you with much. Be faithful in your service in teaching in Sunday School then if God is pleased with your faithfulness he will entrust you with a greater service.

Be faithful in every service commended to you then God will entrust you with dedication. There are some people who think that they cannot serve the church unless they are in authority. One of them may say: "If I were a bishop or an archbishop I would do this and that. If I were a priest I would have corrected the whole of this district, or this country or this town", while he could be remote from the service or his service is a failure. As for you, do not say such things.

Be faithful in your own house then the Holy Spirit will entrust you with the House of God. Do the little that you can. Be faithful in bringing up your children then God will present to you His children to bring up. Most probably it was for this reason, in mentioning the conditions of anointing the clergy, that the Holy Bible says: *"...having faithful children not accused of dissipation or insubordination"* (Titus 1:6), and that the clergyman should be *"one who rules his own house well, having his children in submission with all reverence (for if a man does not know how to rule his own house, how will he take care of the Church of God?)"* (1 Tim.3:4,5).

Therefore, how can he who is incapable of a few things be capable of many? How can he who cannot rule one house be entrusted to rule all the faithful congregation? Faithfulness is tested primarly in the few things, not only in regard to a house or to a class in Sunday School, but there is something prior to all these. It is the faithfulness of the minister regarding his own life and how he rules it. That is why we say:

Be faithful over your own soul then God will entrust you with the souls of others. Test your faithfulness first in ruling your own soul which is with you always and you know all its inward parts and its points of weakness. You can upbraid it and it will obey you. If you are not faithful in ruling your own soul how then can you be trusted to rule others? If you are not able to lead one soul that is within you, how can you lead many other souls? One of the saints said: "He who is not honest over one denarii is a liar to think that he will be honest over a thousand".

The importance lies in faithfulness and not in the

position you occupy. Saint Stephen was not one of the Twelve Apostles, neither was he a bishop of the Church. He was just a deacon. Nevertheless, he was so faithful that many believed through him; the councils of philosophers were brought to shame and he became chief of the Church leaders. In like manner was the deacon Saint Athanasius, the subdeacon Mar Ephraim the Syrian and the cobbler Saint Simeon.

Saint Abba Ruis was faithful with no rank. He was not a deacon nor a subdeacon nor a monk. He was not of the clergy nor of the church servers. Nevertheless, he was faithful in his spiritual life and in his relationship with God, and he became one of the saints of his generation, loved and esteemed by the Pope and Patriarch of his generation. Therefore the importance lies in faithfulness in life and not in status.

What then is your faithfulness in your responsibility, no matter how small it is? The hero of a play is not necessarily a king or chief or leader. He may be a servant yet still the hero, esteemed and appreciated by people because of his honesty in perfecting his role, irrespective of its status.

Therefore, be faithful in the little you have, and know that the man of the two talents received the same blessedness which he of the five talents received because he was parallel in faithfulness. And the blessedness of the Lord centred on the faithfulness and not on the two talents or the five talents (Matt.25:21,23).

David was faithful in shepherding the flock of sheep so God entrusted him to shepherd His people. He was faithful in the little which was the few sheep in the wilderness (1Sam.17:28), for when a lion and a bear attacked one of the flock, he confronted them and saved

the lamb from them. When the Lord saw his faithfulness
he entrusted him to save a whole army from Goliath the
Giant. When he was faithful in confronting Goliath, God
entrusted him with the whole kingdom.

So it should be with you. Enter into this series of
faithfulness.

Be faithful in the house of Potiphar and God will
entrust you with the palace of Pharaoh and the land of
Egypt. Be faithful in the little capabilities you have then
God will entrust you with more and more capabilities. Be
faithful in offering the handful of flour which you have
and the little oil in the jar as the widow of Zarephath was,
then the Lord will entrust you with the bin of flour which
shall not be used up, and the jar of oil which will not run
dry throughout the time of famine (1Kin.17:12,16).

The Will and the Intellect

You may stand despondent before errors that prevail
over you as though they were firmly fixed habits, crying
with the Apostle, saying: *"...but how to perform what is
good I do not find. For the good that I will to do, I do not
do; but the evil I will not to do, that I practise"*
(Rom.7:18,19). What shall I say to you then?

**Be faithful in what is within your will's capability
then God will entrust you with what is beyond your will.**
Be faithful in resisting the wilful sins then God will
entrust you with the resistance of the unintentional sins.
You ask: "What shall I do about the impure dreams
which come to me whilst I am asleep and I am unable to

shun them from myself, and they have become firmly rooted in my subconscious?"

I say to you: Be faithful in restraining your conscious mind then God will entrust you with the control of the subconscious. Be faithful in resisting the errors committed whilst you are awake then God will entrust you with resisting the errors during sleep. Be faithful in guarding your intellect during the day then God will entrust you with purity of intellect during your sleep. If you are circumspect over the purity of your thoughts whilst you are awake then the time will come when your thoughts will be pure whilst you are asleep. Let your thoughts be holy during the day then their sanctity will accompany you during the night.

If you are faithful in resisting the provocations of the senses, God will grant you victory in the noetic warfare because the senses are the doors of the intellect and the causes of thought. If you are faithful in abandoning the causes of the erroneous intellect God will protect you from erroneous thoughts. If you are faithful in fighting the thoughts then God will entrust you with purity of heart which is greater. If you are faithful in keeping this purity then God will entrust you in the Last Day with the crown of righteousness (2Tim.4:8), in the other world where sin is not known.

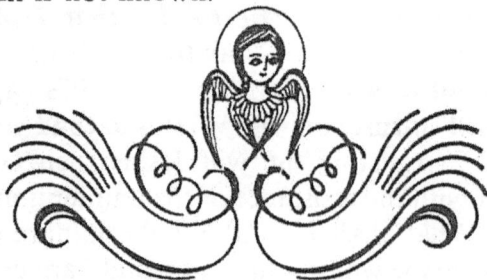

Love

You say: "I want to reach perfect love, to love God with all my heart and with all my might (Deut.6:5) and to love all people even my enemies, and love goodness. Is it feasible that I shall reach this virtue which seems so difficult?" I say to you: Start with the little then you will attain much.

If you are faithful in keeping the virtue of the fear of God then God will entrust you with the virtue of love. This is because *The fear of the Lord is the beginning of wisdom"* (Prov.9:10). If you are faithful in the fear of God and consequently keep His commandments, God will entrust you with the love that casts out fear (1Jn.4:18). Faithfulness in one level is conducive to faithfulness in a higher one. You ask:"And how can I keep the commandments when I love the world and there are some commandments whose contraries my heart craves for?" I say to you: Start with self-coercion. Force yourself to do good.

If you are faithful in self-coercion you will inevitably reach the love of goodness because love for God and for goodness may not be the starting point but is an outcome of a long spiritual endeavour. Therefore force youself to do good. When you practise it you will enjoy it. Then you will love it and you will do it out of love without compelling yourself. In this way God would have entrusted you with much.

Also if you are faithful in loving your brother whom

you have seen you will reach the love of God whom you have not seen (1Jn.4:20). Therefore start with this little which is the love for people then you will reach much which is the love for God. But you may ask: "How can I reach the love of people when they include enemies and opponents? How can I reach the love of enemies?" You reach them through the same rule, that is, by being faithful in the few things.

Be faithful in loving your relatives then you will reach the love of your acquaintances.

Be faithful in loving your acquaintances, then you will love your enemies. Because the heart is used to love there will come a time when hatred will be completely eradicated from it. Then enmity will only be from one side, in your foes and not in you.

The Body and the Spirit

He who is faithful in virtues practised by the body is elevated to virtues of the spirit. **He who is faithful in controlling the body to abstain from food, God will entrust him with controlling the spirit to abstain from sin.** He constrains his tongue to abstain from idle talk, controls his mind to abstain from evil thoughts, and restrains his heart from lust. But he who is not faithful in abstaining from food- and this is a little thing which does not need much effort- how then can he reach abstinence of spirit? Thus said one of the saints:

"Through stillness of body we acquire stillness of soul." Stillness of soul is a great thing which we do not reach unless we are faithful in observing stillness of body. This means that the body should not be engaged in wandering from one subject to another, and the senses should be restrained from vain hearing, looking, touching and smelling.

Also through solemnity of body we attain solemnity of soul. And Through faithfulness in humility of the body we acquire humility of the soul. He who prays with solemnity of body; standing in reverence, lifting his eyes, preserving his senses and his motions, kneeling at the time of kneeling, prostrating at the time of prostration, if he does all these with fidelity, there is no doubt that God will endow him with solemnity of spirit and solemnity of intellect. He who is faithful in his prostrations God will grant him to worship in Spirit and in truth. There is no doubt that he who says the word *Agios* (Holy) whilst bowing down in faith, engenders solemnity in his heart.

Thus we benefit from taking off our shoes when we enter or worship before the Sanctuary. These are physical gestures but if they are performed with loyalty and in faith they transfer the solemnity of the body to the spirit, and the spirit will also worship solemnly. This is due to the correlation of the body and the spirit.

Thus if we are faithful in our physical temple, it will become a temple for God. **And if we are faithful in the material body the Lord will entrust us with the illumined spiritual body in the Day of Resurrection** (1Cor.15:44). If we are faithful in material matters in general God will entrust us with the spiritual matters. Let us take prayer as an example.

Prayer

Someone may ask: "To what extent ought men to pray always and not lose heart (Lk.18:1)? And how can we keep the commandment: *'Pray without ceasing'* (1Thess.5:17)? Is this not too much for us?"

Yes, it is too much if you consider it the starting point. But you start with the little, then God will entrust you with much. **Be faithful in getting used to prayer, then God will entrust you with lengthy prayer.** If you are faithful in the Lord's Prayer and say it with depth, meaning every word you say, there is no doubt that it will open to you doors of contemplation and lead you to many other prayers. If you are faithful in the set prayers, God will entrust you with the prayer of the heart.

The remaining problem before us is the problem of time which is raised by some. We reply that if a person is faithful in prayer during the available time then God will make available for him many other times in which he can pray. But the problem is that we have plenty of time in which we can pray but we waste it vainly and are not faithful in our desire to pray.

Some also raise the question of the levels of prayer and the state of ravishment and theoria and the prayer with tears, and how they can be attained. We reply with the same principle: He who is faithful in the little, God will entrust him with much. **Be faithful in praying ardently and with understanding then God will entrust you with the prayer with tears.** Be faithful in praying

constantly and with love for God then God will entrust
you with the other levels of prayer. They will come
spontaneously without you desiring them as levels
because the subject of levels may entail egoism. The
spiritual life is a spiritual ladder. You cannot reach the
top step unless you pass peacefully through all the
preceding ones.

Examples of Faithfulness

**Be faithful in what is in your hand then God will
entrust you with what is in His hand.** Be faithful in using
your potentials then God will entrust you with potentials
which are not yours. If you perfect walking with the
footmen without getting weary then God will entrust you
with horse racing (Jer. 12:5). If you are faithful in fighting
visible sins God will entrust you with victory over the
hidden sins and the unwitting sins.   '

**If you are faithful to God in your childhood and
adolescence, God will grant you faithfulness in youth
warfare.** If you are faithful in accepting Leah, God will
entrust you to marry Rachel (Gen.29:27). If you have
been faithful in sojourning in the Wilderness of Sinai
God will entrust you with the promised land of Canaan.

**If you are faithful in this limited and short life God
will entrust you with the eternal infinite life.** What is
important is that you should be faithful in everything
your hand touches no matter how small or little it is.
Therefore be faithful in the one talent you have and then

God will entrust you with five talents. Be faithful in the visible matters then He will entrust you with the invisible matters; the things which eye has not seen, nor ear heard, nor have entered into the heart of man (1Cor.2:9).

Be faithful in the fruit of the Spirit then God will entrust you with the gifts of the Spirit. Do not hasten to seek the gifts (1Cor.12) without acquiring the fruit first (Gal.5:22,23) because in the characteristics of the spiritual path the fruit of the Spirit should precede the gifts of the Spirit.

If our father Adam had been faithful in the little, which was not to eat from one of the trees, he would not have gone through all that happened to him. If he had succeeded in passing the test he would have been able to eat of the tree of life.

One of the cannons of monasticism is that he who is faithful in the period of coenobitic life and in acquiring its virutes can then enter the life of solitude if he wishes. One of the monks said to his spiritual father in the monastery: "I want to dwell in solitude because I cannot tolerate the harassment of the brethren". Then the experienced father replied: **"If you cannot forbear the troubles of the brethren in the coenobitic life how then can you forbear the wars of the devils in solitude?"**

The Penitent Thief was faithful during the five hours he spent on the cross, so God admitted him into Paradise.

One of the fathers asked his son to clean a field from thorns. When the son went and found the field full of thorns, he was despondent and slept without doing anything. When his father knew what had happened, he said to him, "My son, everyday clean an area only as big as the size of your bed and there will come a time when the whole field will be clear of all the thorns."

Saint Abba Abraam the Bishop of Fayoum was faithful in the virtue of mercy. He gave whoever asked him and kept nothing of his money for himself but gave it all to the needy. When God saw his great faithfulness he entrusted him with a bigger and greater act of mercy. He endowed him with the gift of healing the sick. Thus Saint Abba Abraam was faithful in the few things.

CHAPTER NINE

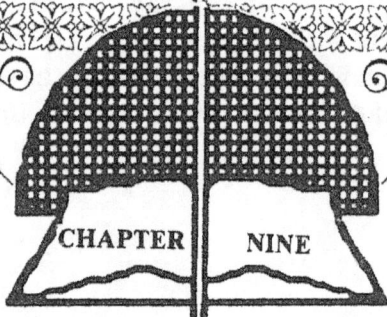

Seriousness and Meticulousness

The Importance of Seriousness

Seriousness is one of the most important characteristics of the spiritual path without which man cannot attain his goal. If we were to ask: **How did the saints reach those high levels in the life of the Spirit?**, the answer would be, because they walked in the spiritual path with utter seriousness. They had a clear line which they designed for their life and they walked along it with unshakeable steadfast hearts, swerving neither to the left nor to the right. They had fixed principles which they adhered to, never allowing the circumstances to hamper their advance.

Thus the saints progressed. Saint Abba Mishael the Hermit walked in monasticism with seriousness from the very first day and was able to become an anchorite when he was seventeen years old. His spiritual father Abba Isaac witnessed the severe strictness with which he treated himself.

Saint Maximos and Saint Domadius reached high levels of spirituality when the beard of one of them had not yet grown. Their prayers were like beams of light ascending to heaven, and that was because they walked seriously in the spiritual path. Saint Tadros the disciple of Abba Pachomius and Saint John the Short became spiritual counsellors in the monastic life in their generations while they were still young men.

What caused Saint Abba Antony the Great to become a monk other than seriousness? He heard the verse which says: *"If you want to be perfect, go, sell what you have and give to the poor, and you will have treasure in heaven; and come, follow Me"* (Matt.19:21). The whole congregation in the church heard this verse at the same time Saint Abba Antony heard it. But he was the only one who rose in complete seriousness and put it into effect. He also heard the words: "If you were a monk you would have gone to the mount in the wilderness because this place is not suitable for monks", and said: "This is God's voice addressing me." He rose with seriousness and entered the depth of the monastic life. Thus he established the life of monasticism with seriousness.

Who of us has this seriousness in carrying out the commandments, meticulously and speedily? Those are examples from the lives of monks. But in the realm of the ministry we can mention as an example Saint John the Baptist whose whole period of service was one year during which he preached repentance and prepared people for the Lord. He was so serious in his service that the Lord said of him: *"...among those born of women there has not risen one greater than John the Baptist"* (Matt.11:11). We also mention the seriousness with which Saint Paul the Apostle walked in the ministry, in that he laboured more abundantly than the rest of the Apostles who preceded him (1Cor.15:10).

Seriousness in life is an indication of manliness and

strong personality. He who is serious in his spirituality respects himself, his principles, his word, and respects the spiritual path in which he walks. He is steadfast and unshakeable. He is like a great ship sailing vigorously in the sea of life towards its goal, and not like a boat hit and tossed about by the waves in every direction.

It is surprising that some people act seriously in their material and worldly affairs, whereas in their spiritual life there is no seriousness at all. They are serious for the sake of earning money or for the sake of gaining promotion or in order to maintain their position or for fear of punishment. As for their spirituality there is no inner impetus prompting them towards seriousness, most probably because the fear of God is not in their hearts or eternity is not before their eyes. This is why they are not committed to a clear spiritual path.

Qualities of the Serious Person

He who is not serious in his spirituality fluctuates up and down, and his walk is unstable. He falls and rises; rises and falls. Sometimes he is fervent in the Spirit and at other times he is listless or utterly alienated from the spiritual life. He sometimes prays and at other times neglects his prayers. He may or may not read the Holy Bible. If he finds time he sits with God, and if he does not find time he is not bothered and faces the matter indifferently. His life and his worship are characterised by indolence, while the Holy Bible says: *"Cursed is he who does the work of the Lord deceitfully"* (Jer.48:10).

Seriousness in the spiritual life is incompatible with negligence, indolence and hesitance or reversion nor does it accept faltering between the love of the world and the love of God. He who is serious is never indifferent over God's prerogatives. He observes God's rights before he requests others to observe them. He walks in God's commandments decisively, meticulously and profoundly, and his obedience to God is without controversy and without negotiation.

Our father Abraham walked in the commandment of obedience with utter seriousness when he took his only son to offer him as a burnt offering to the Lord according to His command. He did not dispute with God nor did he object to His command but he obeyed and his heart remained steadfast and unaltered towards God. Such is the seriousness of obedience. Similarly was the chaste Joseph. He was serious in his obedience to the commandment and in preserving his sanctity even though the matter led to imprisonment. Daniel the Prophet was serious in his worship to the Lord even though it entailed being thrown into the lions' den.

He who is serious has an assiduous heart and does not weaken before external circumstances. John the Baptist was serious in keeping the Lord's commandment when he said to King Herod, *"It is not lawful for you to have your brother's wife"* (Mk.6:18). He said that heedless of imprisonment or martyrdom.

He who is serious does not give excuses for himself nor does he present justifications for his sins. Man should maintain his manliness irrespective of external circumstances. The chaste Joseph was constrained by circumstances, yet he did not succumb or yield to sin with the pretext that he was a slave under the authority of another and that his master's wife was capable of harming him. Daniel the Prophet did not permit himself to eat from the king's delicacies although he was a captive, governed by rules. He was serious in his principles irrespective of the threatening circumstances.

The spiritual person is also serious in his repentance. If he abandons sin, he abandons it seriously without return. He is serious in repulsing the assaults of sins. He is unlike the Hebrews whom Saint Paul upbraided, saying: *"You have not yet resisted to bloodshed, striving against sin"* (Heb.12:4). How deep is the phrase *"to bloodshed"*! He who is serious in his repentance does not postpone his repentance as did Felix the governor (Acts 24:25) and Agrippa (Acts 26:28), but he is like the Prodigal Son who rose immediately and went to his father, repenting with a contrite heart.

The seriousness of repentance appears in the words of the spiritual father who said: *"I cannot recall that the devils caused me to fall into the same sin twice"*, because as long as he recognised the sin he would not return to it again. But he, who after confessing and partaking of the Holy Communion, repeats the same sins and repeats the same confession, is by no means serious in his repentance.

In the famous stories of repentance in the life of saints such as Mary of Egypt, Pelagia and Moses the Black, we notice something important. Repentance was a turning point in their life without return to sin. It was a serious repentance, moving from sin to purity and advancing to sanctity then transcending to perfection. They were transformed from sinners into saints, and became examples of the life of righteousness, a blessing for others and spiritual advisors.

They were serious in denouncing Satan and all his evil deeds. They were serious in their reconciliation with God and in their desire to live in virtue. But those who fall into lapses everyday, depending on the words of the Psalm: *"He has not dealt with us according to our sins, nor punished us according to our iniquities"* (Ps.103:10), are not true repentants, and God's mercy is for those who are serious in their repentance.

He who is serious in his spiritual path is distinguished by continual growth. Seriousness gives him spiritual ardour, and ardour prompts him to advance always. He strives for the sake of purity and perfection to the farthest extent. He gives God all his might and all his resources, all his will and the whole of his heart diligently and persistently. He acts with all the grace given to him, exerting all his efforts without delinquency. He grows everyday in cleaving to God and in abiding in Him. He grows in the depth of the Divine love, and in comprehending and practising virtues. He does not pander to his ego nor does he gratify it or give it excuses for any short-coming. And if his self slackens he forces it to do God's work in order that it may get used to it and perform it with love.

He who is serious is not mindful of his personal desires, but sacrifices every pleasure for the sake of the Lord. **Such were those who were trained on seriousness. They always laboured for the sake of the Lord.** They always sacrificed their comfort for the sake of their spiritual life such as Saint Paul of Tamouh who exerted himself in ascetism in his striving and in subjecting his body to his spirit so much that the Lord said to him, "Enough exertion, My beloved Paul!" Similarly was David the Prophet who said, *"Surely I will not go into* *the chamber of my house, or go up to the comfort of my bed; I will not give sleep to my eyes or slumber to my eyelids, until I find a place for the Lord and a dwelling place for the Mighty God of Jacob"* (Ps.132:3-5). Such is the seriousness of the spiritual life.

He who is serious does not take the hardships he encounters as excuses, but he surmounts them. He does not yield to an obstacle, but struggles and prays, pursuing the ideals, placing before him the words of the Apostle: *"Run in such a way that you may obtain it"* (1Cor.9:24). Thus he is always fervent in the Spirit (Rom.12:11).

As long as the ideals are placed before him he is not satisfied with half solutions nor with passing just one stage of the path, but he continues diligently pressing on towards perfection. Thus he is in continual ascent towards God. Naturally he who advances unceasingly does not relapse or revert. **He takes everything seriously. He is serious in the life of repentance. He does not entertain evil thoughts. He is serious in his spiritual walk and in practising virtue. He is serious in his spiritual practices: he does not breach them whatever the reason may be. He is serious in every word he says and in the vows and pledges he makes before God.** He does not change his mind after taking a vow nor does he negotiate or postpone paying it or try to exchange it with another vow or delay in paying it but with all seriousness, speedily and meticulously he puts it into effect, placing before him the words of the Holy Bible: *"It is better not to vow than to vow and not pay"* (Ecc.5:5). And Japhthah the Gileadite is an explicit example of the seriousness of vows (Judg.11:30-39).

He who is serious in worship is not satisfied with its

outward semblance. But he is concerned with the essence and depth of the spiritual endeavour. That is why he is profound in his worship. He makes sure that it is in faith, with humility and ardour, with solemnity of heart and with understanding, with concentration and heartfelt love for God. He does not allow his intellect to wander here or there, nor does he allow his senses to roam but he effusively prays and contemplates, makes prostrations and fasts. He does not permit his mind to wander outside the church when his body is inside. He is also serious in his service and seriousness always leads to success and perfection. He performs every responsibility commended to him successfully and with perfection whether it be in the church or in his work or in any project placed in his charge.

Temptations of Satan

Satan fights seriousness with every possible means and maybe with convincing text-proofs. He might call it literalism, or submission to the law instead of grace. In reply we say that grace is not an encouragement for slothfulness, indolence or indifference.

Satan may say that seriousness is against flexibility. We say: Flexibility is not a domain for remissness and detachment from every meticulousness and commitment. He may also say that it is against the glorious liberty of the children of God (Rom.8:21). But we say: Freedom is not freedom if it conflicts with a commandment, and true freedom is freedom from sin.

Lastly we say that seriousness is also connected with faithfulness, meticulousness and commitment.

Meticulousness

In order to understand meticulousness at its depth let us presume the following. Suppose an angel declares to a person that his life on earth will end after a week. Undoubtedly during that week the person will walk with every possible meticulousness in order to prepare himself for his eternal life. It is on this criterion that we would like to measure the life of meticulousness.

The Importance of Meticulousness

Meticulousness is one of the most important characteristics of the spiritual path. The spiritual person is meticulous in everything; meticulous in his relationship with God, with people and with himself. He is meticulous in every behaviour, in every word and in every thought. He is meticulous in his senses and feelings, tendencies and appointments, in his time and the regulations that govern him.

He who is meticulous is not only meticulous when he is among people but even more so when he is alone in his private room. Meticulous behaviour is relatively easy in the presence of people because by nature we do not like to be criticized by them or we fear being exposed before them and our defects and faults being revealed to them. That is why the true criterion of our meticulousness appears when we are on our own seen by no one. If we are meticulous when we are alone then this is true and not hypocritical meticulousness. **Meticulousness with the spiritual person becomes a spontaneous part of his nature and not just an attempt or practice.** He is a person who is used to being meticulous in everything by virtue of inner impulses which constitute part of his principles and values. Even if he is not seen by people he likes to be blameless before God who sees him, as well as before the angels and the souls of the saints who see him. Are you meticulous within yourself irrespective of people's judgments?

What is meticulousness?

Meticulousness is circumspection on the least error. It is a sound and discreet heedful behaviour, pursuing the utmost possible perfect position, with no indifference, slackness or negligence.

Meticulousness is a step towards perfection. He who is meticulous by heeding not to fall into small lapses will find it difficult to fall into great ones. He who heeds with all his might not to fall into sins of thoughts will not easily fall into sins of deeds.

Meticulousness and Scruple

Let everyone take heed to differentiate between **meticulousness and scruple.** Scruple is the conscience which sees errors where there are none, or enlarges the assessment of an error, or when a person suffers a smitten conscience and feels guilty unreasonably, or is driven by the love of meticulousness to excess away from truthfulness and condemns righteous behaviour. Scruple is a type of pharisaism and literalism. It is superficial and void of understanding. Its prototype is what the scribes and the pharisees considered precision in consecrating the Sabbath. It was not precision but literalism with no spirit or depth. It was misunderstanding of the commandment.

We reject calling this meticulousness. Meticulousness is the sound spiritual behaviour in the moderate position between indifference and scruple. It reminds us of the scale of the chemist. Every component of the medicine has its precise weight, which if increased or decreased might harm. Likewise is the meticulous spiritual life. He who is meticulous should watch his soul, examine it and not be lenient towards it in anything. He has principles and values which he observes, not allowing himself to descend below their levels because they constitute explicit characteristics of his spiritual path.

The Scope of Meticulousness

He who is meticulous is circumspect over his time, seeing that it is part of his life. He does not spend one minute of it regretfully or uselessly. Consequently he is circumspect in his appointments and in the regime of his life, and does not waste his time vainly. Just as he is meticulous over his own time, he is also cautious about the time of others. You may find a person to whom time is valueless and thinks that other people's time is also valueless to them. Thus he visits, or engages or talks with another person wasting his time whilst the other is too embarrassed to evade him.

As for the meticulous person, he respects his life and his time and respects the life and time of others. He does not allow himself to waste his time in paltry matters nor does he give a conversation or a visit more time than necessary. He is careful to give his spirituality its due time. He is meticulous over the time which he sets apart for his prayers, contemplations, spiritual reading, church going, service and spiritual gatherings. He is also meticulous over the Day of the Lord. He is meticulous over all his spiritual life which is not lost amidst the tumults of engagements. He is meticulous in his prayers, careful that they should be with understanding and fervour, solemnness and depth, faith, love and humility. In his prayers he is neither frivolous nor too hasty to lose their profundity. He is not negligent of the prayers of the hours nor of the psalms. He worships God meticulously. If he makes the sign of the cross he does it accurately with all its spiritual and dogmatic meanings, with all respect, with its spiritual effect and with full trust in its efficacies. With him the sign of the cross is not a mere hasty motion without understanding or reverence.

In entering the church, he is meticulous in his prayer, in his movements, looking neither here nor there. He does not talk with anyone inside the church and does not engage himself with anything other than worship. He does not walk too hastily to lose the reverence of the place but enters the church quietly whilst singing the Psalm, *"But as for me, I will come into Your house in the multitude of Your mercy; in fear of You I will worship toward Your holy temple"* (Ps.5:7). He makes a prostration, then stands in his place with all solemnness, careful in all what he does, preserving his intellect, his senses and his heart so that when the priest says: "Lift up your hearts ", he responds truthfully, saying: "They are with the Lord".

The spiritual person is meticulous in his thoughts. He does not loiter in expelling any erring thought and is always circumspect to keep away idle and worthless thoughts, trying with all his might to make his thoughts pure, communed with God and away from frivolity. He puts before him the words of the Apostle: *"...bringing every thought into captivity to the obedience of Christ"* (2Cor.10:5). But he who entertains thoughts is not meticulous in controlling them.

The spiritual person is also meticulous in his speech. He examines every word before uttering it, with regard to its meaning and suitability to the occasion and the audience. He who talks and regrets what he says is not meticulous in his speech neither is he who is blamed for what he has said and says: "I did not mean it". And he who hurts the feelings of others is also not meticulous.

Rashness in speech is one of the reasons of its lack of meticulousness. Rashness in giving one's own opinion, in judging others, and in giving way to anger exposes the person to errors and causes him to lose the meticulousness of his speech. But he who is slow to speak and examines every word before saying it is meticulous. That is why the Apostle says: *"Therefore, my beloved brethren, let every man be swift to hear, slow to speak, slow to wrath"* (Jas.1:19).

In slowness or discretion, man can control what he wants to say, select the suitable words and be more accurate in his speech. Because after he utters a word he cannot change or withdraw it, as it has already been counted against him!

As a person ought to be meticulous in his speech he ought also to be meticulous in his jokes and laughter. His laughter should not turn into a type of sarcasm or derision, using other people as a subject of humour or mockery to amuse others, thus using laughter as a means of hurting other people's feelings. Everyone has the right to laugh with others but not to laugh at them. Therefore the spiritual person should be meticulous in his jokes and in his laughter so that he may not offend or degrade anybody even if humorously or unintentionally. He should not say any joke he likes unheeding of its effect on his listeners.

The spiritual person should also be meticulous in his criticism and in his blame and admonishing of others. He should not offend in advising nor destroy in upbraiding. Our Master the Lord Jesus Christ warned us, saying: *"And whoever says to his brother, 'Raca!' shall be in danger of the council. But whoever says, 'You fool!' shall*

be in danger of hell fire" (Matt.5:22). And the word
'Raca' is the smallest word of disrespect. How often do
people use the word 'fool' and its various derivatives,
undermining the intelligence and standard of
understanding of others. As for the meticulous they
should not be so. Notice how the Lord Jesus used the
most decent words in his discourse with the Samaritan
woman, leading her to repentance without offending her
at all. If He had used what people call frankness or facing
the erring person, she would have been put off and He
would not have won her soul.

Meticulousness appears in the responsibility
commended to the person whether it be spiritual or
financial or social. His meticulousness leads him to
success and perfection, and to people's respect and trust.
He does not try to give an excuse to justify his position
because a meticulous person considers self-justification
against meticulousness. There are many who are
meticulous in censuring others and not in censuring their
selves with the same measure. With others they are very
strict while with their selves they present many excuses
when the case ought to be the contrary.

Examine yourself with utter meticulousness while
for others try to give excuses. We observe that the Lord
Jesus gave us an example about this in saying about your
sin, *"the plank in your eye"* and about the sin of others,
"the speck in your brother's eye" (Matt.7:3). Thus you
should look at your own mistakes as planks and at
others' as specks. Man's problem in meticulousness is
that he divides sin into small and great and is then slack
with the small. Most probably what he thinks are small
matters are not in fact small. And even if they appear
small, they will turn into great matters eventually. The

spiritual person is not negligent of any error, esteeming it small, because sin is exceedingly sinful for *"the wages of sin is death"*, and it separates him from God because there is no communion of light with darkness (2Cor.6:14). The fault in anything is due to its lack of perfection. A spot on a dress mars its cleanness no matter how small it may be.

The spiritual person is meticulous in resisting sin, cautious not to fall into it. He does not wait until sin approaches and then resists it, but is careful to keep away from it, sealing all the openings so that it does not find access to approach him. If he is attacked by sin he is very meticulous in expelling it. He is meticulous in all his behaviour, listening always to the words of the Apostle, *"See then that you walk circumspectly, not as fools but as wise"* (Eph.5:15). Thus he is meticulous in every work he does; in the work itself, in its means and in its results, whether regarding himself or others. He is even meticulous in the right things that may be unseemly according to the words of the Apostle: *"All things are lawful for me, but all things are not helpful; all things are lawful for me, but all things do not edify"* (1Cor.10:23).

The spiritual person is meticulous in all his movements, in his coming and in his going, in his voice and in his walk. In speaking with an elder person, he is mindful not to raise his voice or interrupt, as the spiritual elder said: "He gently opens and shuts the door". In his speech he is careful that his jokes do not develop into mockery. He is circumspect that he may develop from telling a story to judging, or move from ordering to domineering, or from exemplary to love of praise and talking about the self. Thus he is meticulous not to change from objectivity into subjectivity. Every step has its account. He is not pulled by the common current, does not agree with the common faults and does not move from one place to another without thinking. He is meticulous in his relationship with God, in keeping His commandments, in his promises to Him, in fulfilling his vows, and in giving his tithes and firstfruits. He does not negotiate with God nor does he retract in a covenant he took before Him.

The Devils' Combats

The devil fights meticulousness and calls it rigidity or lack of flexibiity. By this he aims to ensure that the spiritual person will not endure the term 'rigidity', and thence abandon his meticulousness! But what the devil criticizes is the pharisaism and the literalism and not meticulousness. Moreover, flexibility does not mean detachment from values, but it is flexibility in carrying out the commandment and not flexibility in breaking it. So do not let such words stir you to change your principles.

The Life of Victory

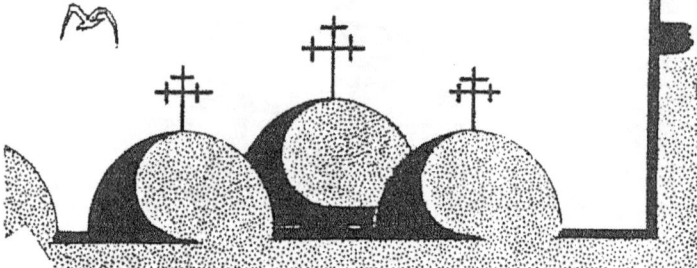

The Life of Victory

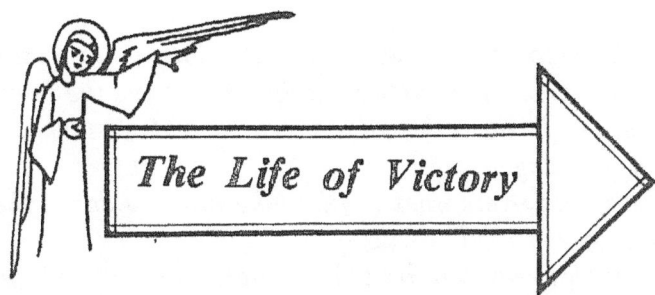

The spiritual man is victorious in all his spiritual warfare: victorious over the self, over material matters and over the devils. As a result of this victory he receives crowns in heaven on that Day. That is why some divide the Church into two; one on earth called the Militant Church and the other in heaven called the Victorious Church which, during the period of striving on earth, fought and prevailed.

The Importance and Blessing of Victory

In the Book of Revelation the Lord explains to us the blessings received by those who prevail. In His messages to the seven churches He repeats each time the words: *"He who overcomes shall be..."* or *"To him who overcomes I will give...",* saying:

"To him who overcomes I will give to eat from the tree of life, which is in the midst of the Paradise of God" (2:7).

"He who overcomes shall not be hurt by the second

death" (2:11).

"He who overcomes shall be clothed in white garments, and I will not blot out his name from the Book of Life; but I will confess his name before My Father and before His angels" (3:5).

"He who overcomes I will make him a pillar in the temple of My God" (3:12).

"To him who overcomes I will grant to sit with Me on My throne, as I also overcame and sat down with My Father on His throne" (3:21).

The Lord prepared all these blessings for those who strive and prevail and live the life of victory. No one was excluded from this rule. Everyone was given the opportunity to strive and prevail in order to be crowned. That is why when Saint Paul's hour of departure arrived, he said effusively: *"I have fought the good fight, I have finished the race, I have kept the faith. Finally there is laid up for me the crown of righteousness, which the Lord, the righteous Judge, will give to me on that Day, and not to me only but also to all who have loved His appearing"* (2Tim.4:7,8).

For this reason God permitted spiritual warfare, temptations and devils. He puts our will to the test to show how far we are worthy of His crowns. Therefore one of the Fathers said: "No one is crowned except he who prevails. No one prevails except he who fights. No one fights except he who has an enemy". And Saint Paul the Apostle said: *"Put on the whole armour of God, that you may be able to stand against the wiles of the devil. For we do not wrestle against flesh and blood, but against principalities, against powers, against the rulers of the darkness of this age, against spiritual hosts of wickedness in the heavenly places"* (Eph.6:11,12).

You Are Not on Your Own in the Combats

God watches over our fights and our victories, and so do the angels and all the souls of the saints. They all look out for our struggles and rejoice when we prevail according to the words of the Holy Bible: *"...there is joy in the presence of the angels of God over one sinner who repents"* (Lk.15:10). God and His angels do not stand silently whilst watching our spiritual warfare, but they provide us with support.

It is true that God permitted the existence of the adversary, yet He did not give him authority over us. He permitted spiritual warfare, yet He gave us power to prevail in them: power from the Holy Spirit, power from the work of grace and power in human nature which has been renewed and regained its former Divine image. God gave us all these powers and He also gave us authority over the devils. In Him we can trample on every power of the adversary. We mention this blessing at the end of the Thanksgiving Prayer w .ich we pray daily, remembering the power which the Lord granted to His pure Apostles as the Gospel according to Saint Luke mentions: *"Behold, I give you authority to trample on serpents and scorpions, and over all the powers of the enemy"* (Lk.10:19).

The phrase *"all the powers of the enemy"* is undoubtedly a comforting phrase if put beside the words *"trample on"*. Therefore the devil is not fearsome as some may think even though he appears as a roaring lion seeking a prey to devour, because the Lord gave us power over him. **God vanquished the devil when He took upon Himself our nature which the devil had previously overcome, and thus gave our nature the spirit of triumph and the spirit of victory.** He also granted us to prevail and showed us the picture of the devil conquered so as not to fear him. Rather He gave our nature the power to cast out demons, and our fathers the Apostles saw how the devils were subject to them in the Name of the Lord (Lk.10:17). How beautiful are the Lord's words about the loss of the devil's power: *"I saw Satan fall like lightning from heaven"* (Lk.10:18). **Therefore do not fear the devils.** They are not more powerful than you so long as you fight them with the full armour of God (Eph.6:11) and with the power of God acting in you and through you. Then they will be subject to you and you will overcome them in your warfare.

God who works in you will conquer them. He said to us: *"In the world you will have tribulation; but be of good cheer, I have overcome the world"* (Jn.16:33). By this He did not only mean His own personal victory over the world but also His victory over the world through us. That is why it was good that Saint Paul said: *"God always leads us in triumph"* (2Cor.2:14). Yes, this is the ever-victorious Christ who overcame the world, overcame Satan and overcame death, and who leads us always in triumph. And as Moses said: *"The Lord will fight for you and you shall hold your peace"* (Ex.14:14). He loves us and He loves that we live the life of victory, and it is He who fights for us. As for our part we say with the Apostle: *"Yet in all these things we are more than conquerors through Him who loved us"* (Rom.8:37). It is true that the Lion of the tribe of Judah, the Root of David, has prevailed (Rev.5:5). And we likewise will prevail so long as we abide in Him taking our power from Him, because He did not give us the spirit of failure but He gave us to sing, saying: *"I can do all things through Christ who strengthens me"* (Phil.4:13).

Our spiritual warfare is not between us and Satan but it is primarily a war waged by Satan against God and His kingdom. And he fights us as part of his fighting against the kingdom of God. This is why God does not leave him to prevail over us. It is His war as is said by David the Prophet: *"...the battle is the Lord's"* (1Sam.17:47). And Moses perceived this fact when he was fighting the Amalekites and said: *"...the Lord will have war with Amalek"* (Ex.17:16).

Do Not Despair Even If You Fall Many Times

Satan wishes continually to instil in your heart the spirit of defeat and the spirit of weakness in order that you may despair and yield to him! Do not believe him. Do not believe him when he keeps telling you that repentance is difficult and the life of righteousness is not practicable in an evil world like ours. Do not believe him if he says to you: "It is futile, your power is feeble and you will surely fall!"

Say to him: "It is not my will but God's work for my sake which matters. And even if I fall I will surely rise, for the Holy Bible says: *'...a righteous man may fall seven times and rise again'* (Prov.24:16). And the prophet said: *'Do not rejoice over me, O my enemy; when I fall I will arise'* (Micah 7:8)!"

After every arising, do not let the fall agitate you, but rejoice that you arose from the fall and be assured that God gives you the power with which you can rise no matter how many times you fall. *"Seven times"* means a full number of falls.

The fall is unlike defeat. It is a mere stage from which you rise victorious at the end. God knows the power of our enemy and the weakness of our nature. That is why He has compassion on our warfare and sends us power to support our weakness, and He helps us to rise. And as we say to Him in the Divine Liturgy: "You showed me how to rise from my fall; You have turned my punishment into salvation. As a true Father You toiled with me, I who fell. You gave me all the medicines conducive to life".

How beautiful are the words of one of the Fathers, who said: **"The soldier who is wounded by the enemy is rewarded with medals and not only the soldier who overcomes and kills his enemies".** So long as the soldier did not flee from the battle but fought and struggled he is rewarded, no matter how much the enemy wounded him. Because this is not defeat; it is striving.

Put before your eyes the words of the Holy Bible: that God *"desires all men to be saved and to come to the knowledge of the truth"* (1Tim.2:4). May you be among those men, and rest assured regarding God's good will. And if God's help delays in reaching you do not despair. **Because although God may come in the fourth watch, yet He will surely come.** Saint Augustine's salvation was after long years of sin, but he received salvation at the end even though it seemed that God's help reached him late! In the same way we speak of Mary of Egypt, Moses the Black, Saul of Tarsus and Arianus the governor of

Ansena.

God went to prepare a place for us and He will come to take us to Him (Jn.14:3). Let us therefore acquire hope in the life of triumph: *"You shall not be afraid of the terror by night, nor of the arrow that flies by day, nor of the pestilence that walks in darkness"* (Ps.91:5,6). But say with David the Prophet: *"Though an army should encamp against me, my heart shall not fear"* (Ps.27:3), *"...though I walk through the valley of the shadow of death, I will fear no evil; for You are with me"* (Ps.23:4). Fill your heart with God's strengthening promises and rest assured that you will definitely prevail.

Causes of Victory

We said that the most important thing is that God fights in you and fights for you. Therefore pour yourself out before him so that He may give you the strength and the victory. Yet along with the help of God you must have complete circumspection, the means to which are:

1. **Keeping away from the causes of sin and escaping from them as best you can.** The angel said to Lot: *"Escape for your life! Do not look behind you nor stay anywhere in the plain"* (Gen.19:17). And Saint Paul the Apostle says to his disciple Timothy: *"Flee also youthful lusts"* (2Tim.2:22). And we have seen a practical example in the chaste Joseph who escaped for his life so that he might not fall. One of the Fathers said: **"He who is near the object of sin fights two wars, one from the outside and another from the inside. But he who is far from it is**

tempted from the inside only". Therefore ascertain from where lapses come to you and abandon their causes, remembering the words of the Holy Bible: *"God divided the light from the darkness", (Gen.1:4) "And if your right hand causes you to sin, cut it off and cast it from you"* (Matt.5:30).

2. **Be meticulous in your life and be on your guard even from the things which seem paltry.** To this effect the Holy Bible tells us: *"Catch us the foxes, the little foxes that spoil the vine"* (Song 2:15). And as one of the Fathers said: "Do not converse with someone whom the devil uses to fight you".

3. **In order to prevail, strive with all your might and do not surrender in the warfare.** Rebut evil thoughts and do not entertain them and do not leave them to increase within you. Resist lusts and bad desires and do not think of putting them into practice, however pressing they may be. Behold Saint Paul the Apostle upbraids the Hebrews saying: *"You have not resisted to bloodshed, striving against sin"* (Heb.12:4). Your escape from sin, your striving against it and your meticulousness are proof that you declare that you are cleaving to God and that your will is good. This encourages grace to work in you.

4. **In order to prevail, you have to strengthen the love of God in your heart by being regular in the means of grace.** Most of those who fall are detached from the means of grace; from prayer, contemplation, reading, fasting, spiritual gatherings, confession and Holy Communion. Cleave to these means of grace. Always be mindful of God and bring into your heart the spiritual feelings which keep you away from sin.

5. **Let your spiritual principles be sound and let your aim be God and His kingdom.** Know that the more

additional aims you have the more they will prevail over your emotions and sever you from God. Then you will not be able to worship two masters: God and your worldly aims. Always try to give your depths to God alone. Whenever other aims begin to creep into your heart, be alert and reject them.

6. **If you want to prevail, preserve continually the humility of your heart.** Humility makes you seek counsel, depending not on your own understanding. Humility makes you acknowledge your sins. Humility gives you contrition of heart and God comes closer to you with His grace and His help. Humility makes you pray asking for God's intervention in your life instead of depending on your intelligence and your capabilities.

7. **Always feel that you are a beginner because this feeling prompts you to advance and grow. Those whose growth ceased, their ardour also ceased, and they became listless and weak and were liable to fall.**

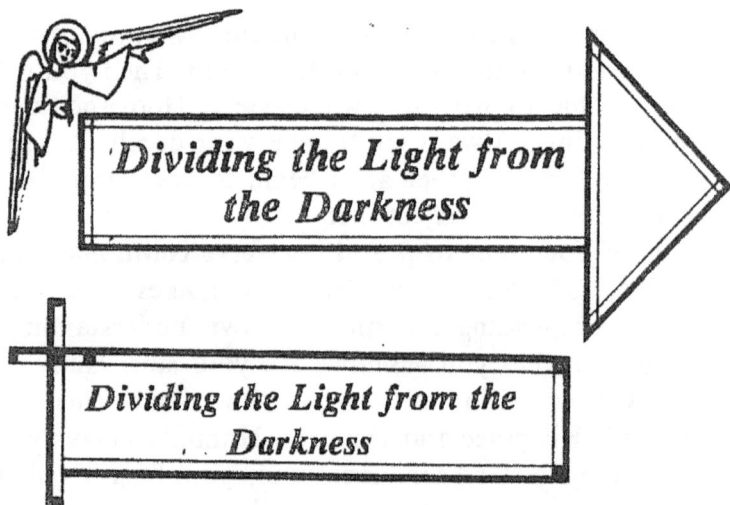

Dividing the Light from the Darkness

Dividing the Light from the Darkness

He who commences the spiritual path with God should cut all his relation with sin and its causes, and always be on his guard against any bad companionship, obeying the words of the Holy Bible: *"For what fellowship has righteousness with lawlessness? And what communion has light with darkness? And what accord has Christ with Belial? Or what part has a believer with an unbeliever"* (2Cor.6:14,15). Therefore, a person must separate himself completely from all the erroneous areas and keep away from the objects of temptation because he cannot combine the love of God with the love of the world.

This point is clear from the beginning of creation as the Divine Inspiration says: *"Then God said: 'Let there be light'; and there was light. And God saw the light, that it was good; and God divided the light from the darkness"* (Gen.1:3,4). This symbolic principle remained as a fixed rule used by God in His dealings with His children in every generation. When evil spread in the world before the Flood, what happened? **The Ark was a symbol of this rule**, for in it Noah and his children were separated from all the wrong companionship in the evil world on which the wrath of God descended, and thus they were saved from perdition.

The same happened with our father Abraham. God said to him at the beginning of his calling: *"Get out of your country, from your kindred and from your father's house, to a land that I will show you"* (Gen.12:1). Thus Abraham was separated from paganism that existed at his time. He was estranged in a holy land in which he was able to worship God and live in righteousness. **When our father Abraham walked against this spiritual rule he suffered in his life.** When he went to the land of Gerar he passed through a severe temptation from Abimelech in which God intervened to save him (Gen.20). The same thing happened previously when he went to Egypt at the time of the famine. He was faced with a trial from Pharaoh but God saved him through miracles (Gen.12:14-20). And from these two events Abraham learnt a lesson.

The same happened but more seriously with Lot in the land of Sodom. His living in an evil environment caused him spiritual trouble. The Apostle Peter said about him: *"...for that righteous man, dwelling among them, tormented his righteous soul from day to day by seeing and hearing their lawless deeds"* (2Pet.2:8). Then the matter developed and he was taken captive, and the country was burnt by the wrath of God. He was saved by a Divine miracle through the intercession of our father Abraham who was remote from the communion of evil and evildoers.

Divine Commandments and Church Rules

God laid down spiritual rules for His people's necessary separation from the erroneous companionship. Among these rules is the forbidding of intermarriage with foreign women. When Solomon the Sage fell into this error, he deviated because the foreign women drew his heart towards worshipping other gods. He built up high places **"for all his foreign wives, who burned incense and sacrificed to their gods"** (1Kin.11:1-8). And Solomon turned to correct this error in many situations in the Book of Proverbs.

Saint Paul the Apostle laid down for us an important spiritual principle in which he said: *"Do not be deceived: 'Evil company corrupts good habits'"* (1Cor.15:33), and: *"...not to keep company with sexually immoral people"* (1Cor.5:9), and: *"...put away from yourselves that wicked person"* (1Cor.5:13). And he said explicitly, *"...not to keep company with anyone named a brother, who is a fornicator, or covetous, or an idolater, or a reviler, or a drunkard, or an extortioner- not even to eat with such a person"* (1Cor.5:11). The same advice is given in the first Psalm: *"Blessed is the man who walks not in the counsel of the ungodly, nor stands in the path of sinners, nor sits in the seat of the scornful"* (Ps.1:1).

Undoubtedly, man is influenced by the surrounding environment. Therefore it is better for him to abandon erroneous spheres. **That was why the Church, during her early generations, used to excommunicate sinners from the communion of the believers,** utterly forbidding their presence inside the church. And church attendance was exclusively for the holy persons. The Church rule of punishment was very severe during the early eras of Christianity. The maximum thing permitted to sinners was to attend the liturgy of catechumens and most probably it was attended by the new believers and not by sinners. They attended only the readings of the epistles, the Acts of the Apostles, the Gospel and the sermon, and then had to leave the church.

This excommunication did not only include those who perverted in their behaviour but also those who deviated in belief, in thought and in dogma. Regarding this Saint John the Beloved said: *"If anyone comes to you and does not bring this doctrine, do not receive him into your house nor greet him; for he who greets him shares in his evil deeds"* (2Jn:10,11). This matter was regarding the innovators and heretics so that they might not spread their opinions among the congregation of believers and influence them. This advice of Saint John may be useful nowadays with those who spread scepticism in religion such as the atheists, Jehovah's Witnesses and whoever innovates ideas contrary to the faith that was once delivered to the saints (Jude 3).

The most famous example of excommunication during the Apostolic Era was the incident of Ananias and Sapphira in which Saint Peter did not accept that the couple lie to the Holy Spirit of God (Acts 5:1-11). Also one of the most important examples is the punishment given by Saint Paul the Apostle to the sinner of Corinth (1Cor.5:1-5).

The oldest example of excommunication was the dismissal of Adam and Eve from Paradise. God separated them from the tree of life and from Paradise and drove them outside. And generally sin is separation from God, from His kingdom and from His angels and saints. The life of righteousness is separation from sin and from the fellowship of sinners.

From baptism the spiritual person begins his first separation from Satan and from sin. In baptism the person openly denounces Satan together with his evil deeds, his unclean spirits, his authority and all the rest of his hypocrisies. He is also separated from his old man. This old man dies in baptism and a new man is born after the image of God. He is also separated from all the sins committed before baptism whether original sin or all actual sins so that man lives a new pure life, abiding in God. Thus the words of the Holy Bible, *"God divided the light from the darkness"* are fulfilled.

A More Serious Separation in Eternity

Just as there is separation here on earth between light and darkness, so there will also be a more profound separation in the life to come. This is obvious from the episode of the rich man and Lazarus the poor when our father Abraham said to the rich man: *"And besides all this, between us and you there is a great gulf fixed, so that those who want to pass from here to you cannot, nor can those from there pass to us"* (Lk.16:26).

On the Day of Judgment there will be a separation between those on the right and those on the left. On the fearful Day of Judgment God will separate the lambs from the goats, and He will separate the wheat from the tares, and He will separate the righteous from the wicked. No longer will both live together as they used to whilst on earth. The righteous will go to the eternal bliss whilst the wicked will go to the fire prepared for Satan and his evil spirits. **The righteous will live in the land of the living whilst the wicked will be thrown into the outer darkness.** Here any sinner can meet any saint and shake hands with him, sit with him and talk with him, and ask his prayers for his sake. But in eternity, sinners will not be able to meet the saints. The rich man cannot sit with Lazarus but watches him from afar, and may not be able to see the righteous at all. **The sinners' deprivation of the communion of the angels and saints will be part of their eternal suffering.** It is a separation between light and darkness according to God's will since Creation.

Therefore if you care for someone's love and continual life with them both here and in the next world, there is but one advice for you: **Live both of you a spiritual life acceptable to God so that you can live together in eternity.** But if each of you walks in a different way regarding righteousness and sanctity you will never meet in eternity. If you both live here a sinful life, your affliction in eternity will occupy you from enjoying each other's company. If you cannot meet with whomever you love in eternity, then at least care for your own eternal life and your love for God, instead of forfeiting your soul.

What Then Should You Do?

If you cannot separate yourself practically from sinners, at least separate yourself from their ways. If you have to live in an unspiritual environment, because such is most of the world, and you cannot leave the world as our teacher Saint Paul said, **if you cannot separate yourself from sinners in body, separate yourself in heart and in mind.** Separate your heart from every evil lust, separate your mind from every erroneous thought, separate your senses as best you can from seeing and listening to what offends you spiritually. Remember the words of Saint Paul the Apostle: *"...and those who use this world as not misusing it"* (1Cor.7:31). Also listen to his saying: *"And do not be conformed to this world"* (Rom.12:2), that is, do not change and become in its image and likeness but be distinguished by your spiritual way as Saint John the Beloved said: *"Whoever has been born of God does not sin, for His seed remains in him; and he cannot sin, because he has been born of God. In this way the children of God and the children of the devil are manifest"* (1Jn.3:9,10).

The children of God have transcended the level of the world and its lusts because they concentrated all their love on God alone, rejecting the position which Elijah criticized when he said: *"How long will you falter between two opinions? If the Lord is God, follow Him; but if Baal then follow him"* (1Kin.18:21). The true believer cannot combine together God and the world, giving one hour to prayer and another to worldly pleasures, without being steadfast in one condition. The Holy Bible says: *"You shall love the Lord your God with all your heart, with all your soul, and with all your might"* (Deut.6:5). The term *"with all"* means that there is no other love beside God competing with Him, and that there is no darkness sharing His marvellous light within you. Your separation from darkness does not only involve the passive side but also involves the positive side according to the words of the Apostle: *"And have no fellowship with the unfruitful works of darkness, but rather expose them"* (Eph.5:11). Exposing darkness means that you do not accept it either inside you or inside anybody else. It means your care for God's kingdom and for its spread. Exposing darkness signifies strength in the heart from within which does not grow weaker before the prince of darkness (Lk.22:53), but it confronts and resists darkness in the same manner as Elijah who stood against King Ahab and the prophets of Baal (1Kin.18), and as John the Baptist who stood against Herod and Herodias (Matt.14:3,4).

You are light. Sin is darkness. And light is capable of extinguishing the darkness. You are light because the Lord Jesus Christ said to us: *"You are the light of the world"* (Matt.5:14), and said afterwards: *"Let your light so shine before men, that they may see your good works and glorify your Father in heaven"* (Matt.5:16). This light of yours when it shines will disperse the darkness from around you. Darkness will not overshadow your light but your light will expel the darkness.

Do you have this spiritual awesomeness which disperses the darkness from around you? Does your mere presence make the people around you unable to utter idle or unsuitable words or behave unfittingly? Does your presence make them feel that you bring the presence of God amongst them? Then they will say to you the sentence they said to that righteous man: "We knew God the day we knew you".

Do you not only separate yourself from the darkness, but even exterminate it? Are you a lamp placed on the lampstand so that there is no darkness because it gives light to all who are in the house (Matt.5:15)? Or are you even a candle which gives light and dispels darkness? Your teaching may be light. This is good, but what is better is that your life itself should be light which gives light to others.

You can never be light unless you love light. You can never disperse darkness unless you hate it from the depth of your heart. Therefore examine your heart thoroughly and make sure of the soundness of its feelings. Disperse from it all darkness. If the love of God enters it all the love of the world and sin will be expelled from it.

You have to trust that sin is darkness. It is enough that you cannot commit sin except in darkness- in secret- without being noticed by people. If you are disclosed to anyone you try to cover it with excuses, justifications or lies, or by referring it to others so that it remains in darkness and no one sees it except you.

So long as God is light, then sin which is darkness separates you from life with God for as the Apostle said: "What communion has light with darkness?" (2Cor.6:14). If the righteous will rise in the last Day with a spiritual illumined body and will shine as snow, and those who turn many to righteousness will shine like the stars forever and ever (Dan.12:3), what shall we say about the resurrection of sinners who were darkness in their life? They will be thrown into the outer darkness and their bodies will never shine. Thus God will have separated in eternity the light from the darkness, not only regarding habitation where the righteous will abide in the illumined city which does not need sun or moon because the glory of God illuminates it, but also regarding the nature of souls. For the souls of the righteous are illumined and the souls of the sinners are dim. The souls of the sinners can never be illumined because they will have been separated from God who is the True Light and because they will live in the outer darkness, and there is no communion for light with darkness.

CHAPTER ELEVEN

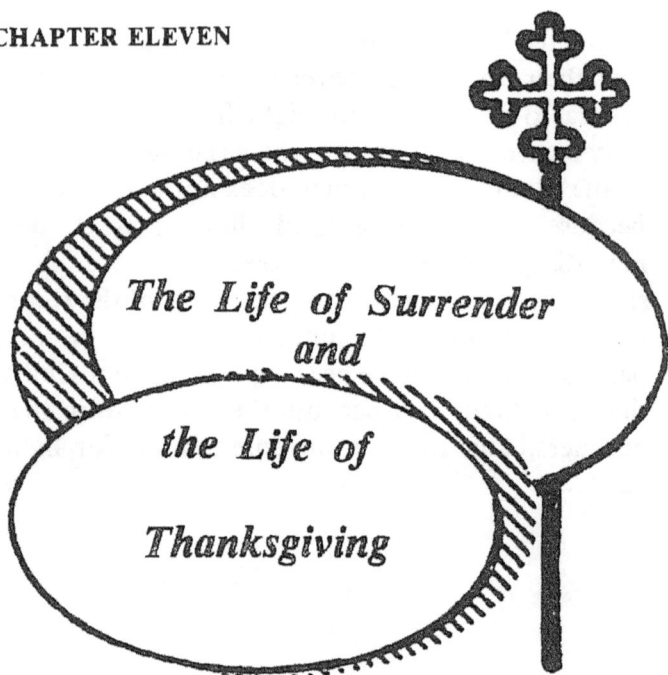

The Life of Surrender and the Life of Thanksgiving

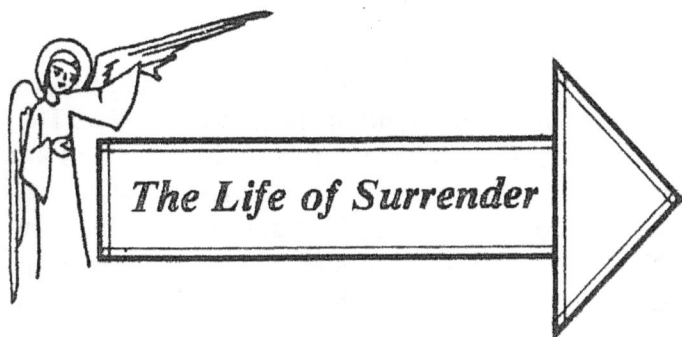

The Life of Surrender

The life of surrender means that you give your life to God commending it into His hands and leaving it there, trusting wholeheartedly that He disposes of it well according to His blessed good Will. So the matter needs trust in God and faith in His love, in His wisdom and in His providence.

Deplorably most people are more confident of themselves, of their intelligence, their reasoning and their human disposition than they are in God. That is why they like to dispose of their own problems. They do not think of recoursing to God and depending utterly on Him as ought to be the case in the life of surrender.

The most perilous thing which causes man to suffer is his independence from God; depending on himself, directed by his ego, his passions and lusts, or by his intellect or by other persons. **Depending on God would then be only partial dependence, within certain limits, which the person does not overstep. Or it would be a superficial dependence void of trust, or a mutable dependence attacked by doubt, fear and lack of confidence.** This reminds me of Saint Peter when he walked on the water with the Lord Jesus Christ. When he feared and lost faith he soon started to fall and deserved the Lord's rebuke: *"O you of little faith, why did you doubt?"* (Matt.14:31).

In contrast were those who walked through the Red Sea with the water surrounding them on either side. They must have entirely surrendered their lives to God and fully trusted in Him. There is a contemplation which says that he who lived the true life of surrender at that time was the first person who put his foot into the water when Moses struck the Sea with his rod, confident that the water would surely divide. Similarly faithful were the people who walked under the cloud not knowing where they were going; but they were confident that God was leading them. **Similar to them was Noah. He entered the Ark with the beasts, leaving the command of the Ark to God alone, trusting that He would bring him out of the Ark to a dry land where the water of the Flood would be completely abated.**

Our father Adam did not walk in the life of surrender when he followed his own desire, his wife and the serpent, independent from God and from His commandment, allowing the lust of knowledge to lead him to ignorance and death! Jonah the Prophet did not walk in the life of surrender when he escaped from God and was angry from His Divine will, even desiring death for himself (Jon.4). The cause of King Saul's perdition was his independence from God, following his own thoughts and whims, and resorting sometimes to the counsel of sorcerers.

The life of surrender is to give your life to God and also to resign to the work of God within you, to the work of grace within you, and to the work of the Holy Spirit and the good will of God.

An exact analogy of the life of surrender is the sheep

with their shepherd. Wherever he leads them, they follow. They are confident in him, trusting in his care and leadership without thinking, without personal opinion, and as we say in the spiritual song: "Where He leads me I will follow". It is utter obedience built on full trust.

Characteristics of the Life of Surrender

The life of surrender is connected with obedience. We mean the true obedience which involves neither grumbling nor duality of will, the obedience in which you obey God with a joyful heart, having no will except His will, saying: "I have no opinion or thought or desire other than to follow You".

The sole reason of falling is the duality, the will of God and the will of man. Our Saviour directed us to the life of surrender in the Lord's Prayer when He taught us to say: *"Your will be done"*. Let Your will be my will. Let my will be Your will. Do not allow His will to be other than your will. If man lives the life of oneness of will he will not err because he will then be in fellowship with the Holy Spirit. He will not resist the Spirit neither will he act obstinately against the will of God. This is one of the fruits of the life of surrender.

Accordingly, sin is a type of obstinacy which does not conform with the life of surrender. Also he who surrenders his life to God *"cannot sin, because he has been born of God"* (1Jn.3:9,10) and *"the wicked one does not touch him"* (1Jn.5:18).

He who lives the life of surrender gives God

everything, gives Him his heart and mind, his senses and desires, his feelings and emotions, trying not to interfere in the work of God. This is the entire surrender by which alone the faithful can cry out with Saint Paul, saying: *"It is no longer I who live, but Christ lives in me"* (Gal.2:20). This is he who has crucified himself completely and no longer has an ego resisting the will of God.

He who lives the life of surrender asks God in every matter: *"Lord, what do You want me to do?"* (Acts 9:6). I do not choose for myself but I always want what You choose for me. Because if I choose for myself I may err in my choice but You know what is good for me. I do not choose for myself because I do not trust my own wisdom. How truthful are the words of the Holy Bible: *"...and lean not on your own understanding"* (Prov.3:5) and: *"There is a way that seems right to a man, but its end is the way of death"* (Prov.14:12,16:25). That is why I surrender the matter and leave it to Your Divine wisdom because You, Lord, see what I cannot see and know what I do not know. You perceive what is good for me and You lead me to green pastures and to the sources of living water.

Therefore the life of surrender should be built on humility and meekness of heart, and on vanquishing the self. The self which trusts in its own understanding and capabilities finds it difficult to live the life of surrender. Those who question all God's purposes and all his works with them and who take the work of God as a domain for discussion and debate cannot reach the life of surrender; they are called rationalists.

Abraham the Patriarch lived the life of surrender when he left his kindred and when he agreed to offer his son as a burnt offering to God. He left his country and his tribe not knowing where he was going. But he had surrendered his life to God to lead him wherever He willed and to lodge him wherever He willed. He also took his only son to offer him as a burnt offering, commending the matter to the Almighty who is able to raise the dead to life (Heb.11:8,9,17-19).

He who lives the life of surrender abandons to God the aim and the means and also the result. God chooses for him the path and the method and every result that comes from Him is acceptable. That is why he lives in continual joy and contentment. Sadness arises if the person defines an aim for himself and it is not fulfilled. But he who lives in utter surrender to God does not define aims for himself because he abandoned to God the direction of his way, as Jeremiah the Prophet said, *"O Lord, I know the way of man is not in himself; it is not in man who walks to direct his own steps"* (Jer.10:23).

He who surrenders his ways to the Lord never worries because he is confident that God will prosper his way, whereas he who leads his own self is prone to worrying. Saint Paul surrendered his life to God. That was why he was singing and praising God even in prison (Acts 16:25). There was nothing which disturbed him and he wrote some of his epistles whilst he was a prisoner for the Lord. Peter the Apostle slept soundly because he surrendered his life to God whilst death was awaiting him the following day (Acts 12:6-19).

The life of surrender leads to confidence even in the most critical moments. It reminds me of the confident patient who lies down quietly in surrender resigning his body to the scalpel of the surgeon. In his sleep and surrender he does not try to ask the surgeon what he is going to do with him. It is sufficient for him that he is in honest hands wishing him good. It is enough for him that he trusts in this hand.

Such were all those who followed God in utter abandonment. They did not question Him nor did they debate with Him, as happened in the calling of our fathers the Apostles. When the Divine call reached Matthew, in the place of tax collection, he left everything without asking where he was going. Peter, Andrew, John and his brother James left their fishing nets and went after Christ the Lord, not knowing where they were going. They did not ask. Such was the life of surrender. **That is why it was good that God chose those who lived the life of surrender.** He knew that they had meek and ready hearts, simple and trusting hearts which would not try to scrutinize obstinately under the presumption of wisdom and prudence. That is why the Lord Jesus Christ said: *"I praise You, Father, Lord of heaven and earth, that You have hidden these things from the wise and prudent and revealed them to babes"* (Lk.10:21), that is, to the meek.

It is as though the faithful person says to God in all his problems: **"I have placed my problems before You, Lord. I fasted and prayed for them and commended them to You trusting that You will work. How? When? I do not know but I am persuaded that You will definitely do good. I will see Your work now or after a while. I see it through faith, love and trust, and through my long experience with You under Your providence".**

This is how man should behave in the life of surrender and he should not concern himself with time. God will work in the time He deems appropriate and beneficial, although it may appear to you that He tarries, because this delay is a relative matter depending on man's way of thinking. In the life of surrender leave time to God and do not fix dates for Him because He knows His work better than you and He knows more than you about the good time.

Trust in God's work even though Satan attacks you with despondency and even though he says to you in wicked rejoicing: "There is no use". So long as you have surrendered your problems to God, then you have placed them into the hands of the Omnipotent, the Lover of Mankind, the Benevolent, the All-Wise and the Omniscient, who carved you on the palm of His hand.

These beautiful attributes of God call you the more to the life of surrender and trust, irrespective of the obstacles that arise before you. God is invariable and His promises are unfailing, His wisdom is the same and His love is the same even though your problem appears stagnant before you. In the life of surrender do not depend upon your senses nor upon your own comprehension. If you pray to God for something, be assured that He has started to work for your sake from the moment He heard you and even before.

The Apostles walked in the life of surrender in their preaching and in their ministry. They went to countries they had never seen before and whose languages they had never heard. They went to countries where there were no churches, no believers and no resources. Yet in the life of surrender they were confident that God would dispose of the ministry and prosper it. It did not concern them how.

In the life of surrener, our fathers the hermit monks lived without human sustenance. They lived wandering in the wilderness and deserted places. Many of them spent tens of years without seeing the face of a human being. In spite of that they were joyful in their lives which they abandoned to the Lord. They and the generations witnessed how God sustained them spiritually and physically in their life of surrender. **He who lives in utter surrender to God has no cares and no worries.** He has placed all his cares upon God since he commended to Him his whole life and so no longer does he worry, because He who cares for everything takes care of him as well. So long as your heavenly Father knows all your needs and as long as He is your Shepherd and you shall not want then why should you worry?

Do not worry about tomorrow, for tomorrow will worry about itself (Matt. 6:34). **The God of tomorrow is He who disposes of it as He disposed of yesterday and the day before.** It is beautiful to know that John the Baptist was taken by an angel from his childhood to the wilderness to be saved, and that Philip after baptizing the Ethiopian eunuch was carried by the Spirit of God to Azotus (Acts 8:39,40). And Saint Macarius the Great when he was exhausted on his way in the wilderness said, "You know, Lord, that I have no more strength", and immediately found himself in Scetis.

The Spirit of God who led our fathers in the past is able to lead you also if you abandon your life to Him. Therefore enter into the life of surrender so that you can also enter into the life of experience and feel the hand of God in your life. Those who lived the life of surrender experienced the Lord and tasted Him. Their faith was strengthened and they entered deeper into the life of surrender. The life of surrender led them everyday to a new experience and the life of experience confirmed them in the life of surrender. **Thus the more their surrender to God increased the more experienced they became. Through experience their faith was reinforced** which in turn enhanced their surrender. One grace led them to another.

Through surrender you live at peace but the multitude of cares are accompanied by abundance of worries. Until when will you bend your back, carrying the burden of worries? Lay them before the Lord. Did He not say: *"Come to Me, all you who labour and are heavy laden, and I will give you rest"* (Matt.11:28)? **Is it too difficult for God, who has carried the burden of all the world from Adam to the end of all ages, to carry your burden?**

There is a person who dwells in the church disturbed, overburdened with cares. Instead of leaving God to carry his burden, he carries, as it were, God's burden. Why do you distress yourself, my son? Why do you trouble your soul by talking much about your burden? surrender the matter to God who will carry you and the Church, carry all your burden and her burden, then you shall not worry.

It is good to experience God, then you will talk about Him to your children, your grandchildren and your spiritual children. You will not only tell them about the God of books but about the God of experience, of fellowship, Whom you have tasted, the God of every day and of every moment and of every event. You will tell them about God who never forsakes His children, of Whom David the Prophet said: *"When my father and my mother forsake me, then the Lord will take care of me"* (Ps.27:10).

Wretched are those who have not tasted the Lord. How can you taste Him? By experience. How can you experience Him? By entering into the life of surrender. Give to Him your life like a child who gives his hand to his father to lead him through the crowds or like an infant who clings to his mother's shoulder, feeling whilst at her shoulder that he is wholly secure, comfortable and at peace.

Let us then return to the life of spiritual childhood, in its simplicity and its surrendering, its trust and its peace, for: *"...unless you are converted and become as little children, you will by no means enter the kingdom of heaven"* (Matt.18:3). The most distinguished quality of little children is their surrendering; they are not too sure of themselves as much as they are of their guardian, father or teacher.

In the life of surrender do not argue and do not doubt, but trust that God takes care of you. Experience the life of surrender and all the joy, confidence and peace it entails. Acquire a spiritual experience by abandoning your life to the Lord.

One of the saints contemplated the verse: *"We have left all and followed You"*, saying: "The things we left are our personal desires and our wills".

Pray, saying, "Lord, I have kept vigil all night and did not catch anything, but through the life of surrender, in Your name I will lay down the nets, confident that they will be full of fish. The God of the sea will fill them".

The Life of Thanksgiving

What shall we say in our prayers to God on the occasion of approaching a New Year? People are used to praying for their needs and this is not wrong, but it is wrong that only a few give thanks to God for His former bounty. And if they do, their thanks is paltry compared to their requests, so the request overwhelms the thanks. One of the spiritual fathers said: **"There is no gift without increase except the one which lacks acknowledgement"**. That is why I would like in this treatise to concentrate on the subject of thanksgiving so that it may be a prominent element in our prayer on New Year's Eve because it is shameful that every year we pray asking for new things without giving thanks for what we have already received.

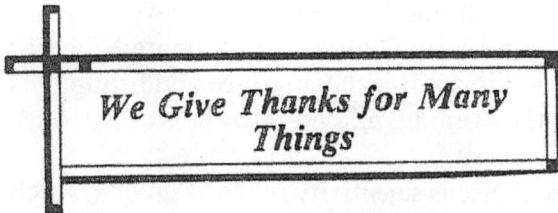

We Give Thanks for Many Things

Give thanks to God for His bounty which He conferred upon you and upon all your acquaintances and your dear friends and for His bounty for the whole Church and for the whole society in which you live. Undoubtedly you will find many bright points for which you need to offer thanks. At least from now on, sit alone with yourself and try to remember in detail all that God has done for you and for those whom you love, not only in the past year but also in previous years or rather in the whole of your life. Thank God because He did not deal with you according to your manner with Him and because He has not punished you for your many sins which you are aware of. But He rather covered your sins and sustained you, opened His house for you and gave you His Mysteries. Do not think that your thanks to God are only for the miracles He has wrought for you but your thanks to Him are for everything. There are minute details in your life that require you to offer thanks and which you might have overlooked.

What Does the Church Teach Us?

The holy Church teaches us to give thanks for things which we may never have thought of. The prayer books remind us of these things. We say in the Eleventh Hour Prayer: "We thank You, O our compassionate King, for You granted us to pass this day in peace and brought us thankfully to the evening, and counted us worthy to see the light until sunset".

What a marvellous sensitivity in thanksgiving which the Church teaches us! She also teaches us to say in the First Hour Prayer: "We thank You, O King of Ages, for You granted us to pass the night peacefully and brought us to the beginning of this day." We thank God for every minute we live. It is a gift from God; it is a chance from

God endowed upon us to do good. Rather, our standing in prayer is a matter we thank God for because He gave us the blessing to talk with Him and gave us the grace with which we detach ourselves from all worldliness and stand before Him, especially on holy occasions.

The Church teaches us to say in the Third Hour Prayer: "We thank You for You called us to prayer in the holy hour in which you poured out Your Holy Spirit...". The phrase "called us" means that we feel that it is the grace of God that impelled us to pray and assisted us to complete the prayer. It is not just the inclination of our human will which, if left by itself, might not have led us to pray.

The Church teaches us to begin every prayer with thanksgiving not only in the Agpeya (the Prayer Book of the Hours) but also in the Divine Liturgy and in all the Church Sacraments. Even in Requiems when we pray for those who departed this world, despite our great love for them, we also begin our prayer with thanksgiving.

We say in the Thanksgiving Prayer: "We thank You for all thigs, in all circumstances, and at all times". It is a prayer of utter abandonment to God, feeling that *"all things work together for good to those who love God"* (Rom.8:28). Most probably this phrase is taken from the words of the Holy Bible: *"giving thanks always for all things to God"* (Eph.5:20).

It is a lesson for those who incline to love the life of grumbling, discontentment and resentment, whereas in the life of faith we give thanks for everything, saying, "We give thanks no matter what happens to us - because all things work together for good".

We Give Thanks for the Bounty and the Affliction

The majority of people give thanks only for the bounty. Few are those who give thanks in time of affliction. He who gives thanks in tribulation is the open-hearted who is not agitated by tribulation. He who gives thanks is he who loves God, who cannot grumble at anything which God permitted trusting in His goodness, providence and care, and feeling that the affliction will definitely end in good.

A higher level than giving thanks in tribulation is giving thanks for the tribulation. Giving thanks in tribulation comes under the virtue of patient endurance or the virtue of trust, feeling that it is an affliction, but we should also give thanks for the tribulation because if God accepted it for us why do we not accept it for ourselves? Giving thanks for the affliction means love of the affliction and the feeling that it is a blessing and not an affliction. An example of this is the disciples who, after having been put in prison, whipped and released, *"departed from the presence of the council, rejoicing that they were counted worthy to suffer shame for His name"* (Acts 5:41). Another example of this type is the saying of Saint James the Apostle: *"My brethren, count it all joy when you fall into various trials"* (Jas.1:2).

Naturally, he who gives thanks for the affliction gives thanks for the benefits. And here we ask: Do you thank God for all His benefits? Or are there some which have gone unnoticed or have been forgotten and which you do not give thanks for?

How numerous are God's benefits which He conferred upon you and which you do not know of! Most probably you give thanks to God for saving you from a certain tribulation which you know of. But there are other adversities which God prevented whilst they were on their way to you. Intrigues might have been plotted against you of which you were unaware, and God prevented them from troubling you and He foiled them. You do not give thanks for them because you do not know of them. A sin might have been creeping on its way towards you to make you fall and God prevented it from approaching you. The devil might have been about to entice you to destroy your faith and the Lord rebuked him and he did not approach you at all. You did not know, so you do not give thanks.

As God commanded us to do good in secret, He likewise does good for us in secret. The manifested good which He does for us is but to make us feel His love. We love Him because He first loved us. That is why, no matter how much we thank God, we can not give Him His due of thankfulness. It is enough that He made us temples for His Holy Spirit making His Spirit dwell in us and work in us (1Cor.3:16), (1Cor.6:19). It is enough that He permitted to be our Father and we His children. About this matter, Saint John the Apostle said: *"Behold what manner of love the Father has bestowed on us, that we should be called children of God"* (1Jn.3:1).

Therefore may we give thanks for all things: for the spiritual blessings, for the material blessings, for the blessings we see and for the blessings we do not see. May we also give thanks for the affliction because it is a blessing too. You may pray: "I thank you Lord from the inner depths of my heart for this illness because it drew me closer to you, it made me return to my prayers, it made me examine myself and blame her for her sins. Thank you Lord for the illness because of the love of many which enveloped me in my illness. I thank you also for this illness because it gave me a chance to sit alone with You, it gave me the blessing of suffering and made me feel my previous delinquency in visiting the sick. It rather induced me to prepare for my eternity. How numerous are the blessings of this illness, and how appropriate that I should give thanks for it!"

Hindrances to Thanksgiving

1. Sometimes we do not give thanks because we do not see the bright points in our life and only concentrate on the troubles. Our concentration on the troubles brings us sadness, anxiety, grumbling and pessimism which do not give a chance for thanksgiving. I want you to begin your New Year with joy and with a smile. So remember all the joyful things in your life and thank God for them.

2. We do not give thanks because we do not attribute the joyful things in our lives to God. If we succeed we give the credit to our intelligence or to our teachers' efforts or to the easiness of the examinations. Thus God's assistance disappears. Also if we recover from an illness we give the credit to the doctors. If we succeed in our profession we give the credit to our capabilities and our efficiency. If we are saved from an

accident we give the credit to the cleverness of the driver. Consequently God disappears from the causes of our joys and we do not give Him thanks for all things.

3. Sometimes we do not give thanks for something unless we lose it or are deprived of it. We do not feel the grace we are in unless it disappears from us. We do not thank God for our parents nor feel their blessings unless one of them dies. We do not give thanks for our health nor do we appreciate it unless we fall ill. We do not feel the blessing of the light in the room unless the electricity is cut off.

4. Sometimes we do not give thanks because the matter is too paltry to give thanks for, or this is how we see it. Here we mention the words of one of the spiritual fathers: "He who does not give thanks for the little is a liar to say that he gives thanks for much". We do not give thanks for something because it is a natural or normal thing which is not worthy of thanksgiving. Why do we not thank God for the beautiful Nature? Why do we not thank Him for the weather when it is bright? Should we wait until it is dull and feel that we have lost something?

5. We often rejoice over the blessing and are sufficed with the joy and do not give thanks. We rejoice over the good we are in without giving thanks for this good, such as a student who rejoices over his success or a young lady over her engagement, or an employee over his promotion without offering thanks to God. God is not in need of our thanksgiving but we are. Why? Because through thanksgiving we remember God's bounty and love for us. This augments the depth of our relationship with Him and makes us love Him. This is beneficial for us spiritually. Also, thanksgiving is an indication of purity of heart because without it there is no gratitude or

appreciation to God who loves us.

6. We sometimes do not give thanks because we are not used to it in our lives. If we do not thank our brethren for the favours they offer us, naturally we will not give thanks to God either. The words which the Apostle said about love that *"he who does not love his brother whom he has seen, how can he love God whom he has not seen?"* (1Jn.4:20), apply also to thanksgiving.

Therefore accustom yourself to thanking others for everything they do for you no matter how small it is. Then say: "Thank You Lord because You sent me someone to help me and gave them strength to serve me". Thus you thank God and people simultaneously. You thank your brother because he was the visible direct medium and thank God because He, in an invisible way, paved all these things for you.

7. Sometimes we do not give thanks because of our selfishness. We think only of ourselves. If the self receives, it is satisfied and does not think of the hand that gave it. It is like a hungry person before whom food is placed, and who starts gulping it down without thinking of the one who placed it before him nor of thanking him. We are also preoccupied with ourselves when we receive, not looking at the face of the giver, like the person before whom the doors of earning money are opened. He starts to be engaged in amassing money and increasing it and does not find one second in which to thank Him who conferred upon him all this.

8. We do not give thanks because we are forgetful, forgetful of what we receive and forgetful of giving thanks. If we train ourselves on thanksgiving it will drill in our souls unforgettable things, that every good thing is a gift from God: life, health, work, money, and so on. So

long as they are gifts then we have to offer thanks for them to the Giver.

9. Sometimes we do not give thanks for things with the pretext that they are intrinsic matters. Here we confuse between the innate qualities and gifts. You think well and do not give thanks for the gift of reason which God endowed upon you. In fact, He is the One who also granted you intelligence and understanding yet you do not say with the Psalmist: *"I will bless the Lord who has given me counsel"* (Ps.16:7). Do not think that intelligence is something intrinsic. It is a gift from God, for which you must thank Him. The same applies to all other gifts and to all your spiritual life.

10. Sometimes we do not give thanks because we cannot perceive God's wisdom. Many things pass us by and for which we do not give thanks. But on the contrary we may be annoyed over them or grumble because of them. All this is because we do not perceive God's wisdom in them. If we did we would have given many thanks to God. The fault lies in us. We have eyes but they cannot see the good in all the events and matters that pass us by. Selling the chaste Joseph and throwing him in prison concealed good things behind them which Joseph might not have perceived at the time nor did he refer to them until they happened.

11. Sometimes we do not give thanks for the good things because we draw comparison. We do not give thanks to God for what He gives us because we see that others have more or better things than us, or because others received the same as us but unworthily.

Compare yourself with whoever is below you and then you will thank God. Do not compare yourself with whoever is above you lest you rebel. Such as a millionaire who does not thank God because there are others who possess more than he. Whenever he compares himself with them he is displeased and feels that what he has is little and trifling and is not worthy of any thanksgiving. This leads us to a similar point.

12. There is someone who does not give thanks because of ambition. He always has hopes higher than his standard, and has desires beyond his ability. The more he walks towards that ambition the less paltry he considers what he has, and he ceases to give thanks for it.

Moderate ambition not inspired by the lusts of the world is not a sin but ambition which hinders thanksgiving is. Thank God for what you have that He may give you more. Ambition should not make you belittle what God granted you. If your ambition is to be a professor at university it does not mean that you should not thank God who made you a teacher and assisted you to reach the post of lecturer. Many are those who are victims of the wrong ambition because of which they are oblivious of God's bounties and live in sorrow and grumbling. As for the spiritual ambition it has no victims if its possessors live in humility and thankfulness to God, desiring to be filled with His love.

13. Sometimes people do not give thanks because they are accustomed to grumbling, covetousness and love of the world. Such persons live in sin and have no relationship with God and do not acknowledge His bounties. All they care for is worldly pleasures and as the Holy Bible says: *"All the rivers run into the sea, yet the sea is not full"* (Ecc.1:7). Rejoice over what you have in your hand and give thanks to God and do not say: "The fullness of my hand is not enough. I want the fullness of my pockets and my stores!" Greediness hinders

thanksgiving. Undoubtedly, if man is not used to the life of contentment it is difficult for him to attain the life of thanksgiving.

14. Sometimes ingratitude is due to weakness in the whole spiritual life. For example, a person does not thank God because he has no relationship with Him whatsoever, no thanksgiving, no prayer, no Bible reading, no spiritual gatherings and no communion with God at all. Such people need to commence life with God. Then, when they thank God who imparted to them the blessing of knowing Him, they will thank Him for all other things.

Virtues Pertaining to Thanksgiving

Virtues are connected with one another. Thanksgiving is connected with contentment. Those who are content are thankful.

Thanksgiving is connected also with humility. The humble person feels that he deserves nothing. Therefore he gives thanks for everything however small it may be.

Thanksgiving is connected with faith. Man by faith is confident that God is the One who keeps, sustains and loves, and that He turns everything into good. That is why he gives thanks for everything.

Thanksgiving is connected with joy and peace; they are born of it. The more a person gives thanks the more his heart is filled with joy and peace. And if his heart is full of peace and joy then he will give thanks.

The thankful person is saved from illnesses and from the many problems which encompass the grumbling and the unthankful. Let us start this year with thanksgiving. May it be a blessed year for us, for the Church, for our country and for the whole world.

The Narrow Gate

CHAPTER TWELVE

What Are These
Tribulations?

Self-Denial

Toil for the Sake
of God

The Narrow Gate
Is For All

Assessing
Tribulations

The Narrow Gate

One of the characteristics of the spiritual path is that you enter it by the narrow gate. This is the teaching of the Lord Himself: *"Enter by the narrow gate, for wide is the gate and broad is the way that leads to destruction, and there are many who go in by it. Because narrow is the gate and difficult is the way which leads to life, and there are few who find it"* (Matt.7:13,14).

Therefore, among the characteristics of the spiritual path are to toil for the sake of the Lord, to sacrifice, to forbear and not to pursue your comfort in this world, but to walk in the rites of Lazarus the Poor and not that of his rich fellow.

The tribulations which you endure are indication that you are serious in your love for God and that you are ready to expend everything for His sake. This present life is only a time of trial: Do you prefer your spirituality, your eternity and your relationship with God to all else? Are you prepared to pay the price? The tribulation here is to test you, to show how far you are cleaving to God. Tribulation here appears as a necessary experience and a fundamental characteristic of the spiritual path. Because what right do you have to be rewarded in heaven and receive crowns if you have lived in luxury on earth? Do you wish to make the best of both worlds, having enjoyment on earth and felicity in heaven? Do you not in this way, expose yourself to the words of our father Abraham: *"Son, remember that in your lifetime you received your good things"* (Lk.16:25)?

Therefore if you walk in God's path and find everything easy before you and you are at complete ease, with no tribulation and no toil, ask yourself: "Have I missed the way? Surely I must have because the way of the Lord is not this easy with no toil. Is there no devil to wage his war against me? Are there no obstacles from the world, from materials and from the flesh? Is there no resistance from the adversaries of good? **No doubt if my behaviour displeased Satan he would by no means have left me in comfort! Why then is he not attacking me?"**

The matter makes one suspect! Who of the saints lived all his life at ease without trouble? Not one of them. All the saints entered by the narrow gate for the sake of their love for God, for it had been granted to them not only to believe in Him, but also to suffer for His sake (Phil.1:29). **That is why these tribulations whisper in your ears, saying: "Be confident**, you are walking in the right path".** Thus rejoice, be glad and rest assured whenever you encounter a tribulation in the way of the Lord because such are its characteristics.

What Are These Tribulations?

Firstly, they are the resistance of this material body against the desires of the Spirit because *"the flesh lusts against the Spirit, and the Spirit against the flesh"* (Gal.5:17). Thus the spiritual person enters into a struggle to bring the body under subjection, as Saint Paul the Apostle said: *"But I discipline my body and bring it into subjection"* (1Cor.9:27). This discipline may take a longer or shorter time depending on the severity or mildness of the warfare.

The subjection of the body is a narrow gate by which you enter and involves various spiritual practices. We mention that our forefathers Adam and Eve did not enter by this gate when they ate of the tree. And Esau, Jacob's brother, did not enter by it either when he sold his birthright (Gen.25:34). Also the children of Israel refused to enter by this narrow gate when they grumbled over the heavenly food and craved for meat (Num.11:4).

Contrary to those was Daniel the Prophet when he purposed in his heart that he would not defile himself with the portion of the king's delicacies, preferring, together with the three saintly youths, to eat vegetables (Dan.1:8,12).

For this reason spiritual aspirants enter into the practice of fasting and vigil. By fasting they resist the lust of the flesh for food, and by vigils they resist the lust of the body for rest and sleep. They preserve themselves watchful through the works of prayer and contemplation. The outward semblance of fasting does not suffice them, but they foremost concern themselves with subjecting the body to co-work with the spirit. So they join the body in the work of the spirit through prostrations so that the body shows solemnity and joins with the spirit in revering and glorifying God. Thus the whole of man, body and spirit, worship God.

One of the important point in submitting the body is to preserve its purity and chastity. Those who walk in the passions of the flesh enter by the wide gate; the gate of bodily pleasures of which Solomon the Sage said: *"Whatever my eyes desired I did not keep from them. I did not withhold my heart from any pleasure"* (Ecc.2:10). These pleasures are rejected by the spiritual persons who struggle to the point of bloodshed striving against sin (Heb.12:4).

In submitting the body, the spiritual aspirants resist the sensual pleasures. The senses which incline to satisfy the desires of seeing, hearing and tasting are restrained by the spiritual person, curbed and brought under surveillance. Thus the spiritual person strives, giving the body no comfort, but as the Apostle says: *"And everyone who competes for the prize is temperate in all things"* (1Cor.9:25).

Self-restraint is entering by the narrow gate. The ordinary person tries to gratify his whims whereas the spiritual person watches over the self and controls it well, disciplines his body and brings it, together with his soul, under surveillance. He does not succumb either his soul's desires or to the lust of the flesh. The Apostle considered the lust of the flesh part of the love of the world (1Jn.2:16), and the love of the world is enmity with God (Jas.4:4). Therefore one of the features of entering by the narrow gate is curbing man's desires so that they do not deviate, and from the positive side it is entering into the love of God, longing for His kingdom and adorning the body with everything befitting the temple of the Holy Spirit (1Cor.6:19).

Self-Denial

In this respect the Lord Jesus Christ said: *"If anyone desires to come after Me, let him deny himself, and take up his cross, and follow Me"* (Matt.16:24). **The person has to place God the prime of his concerns, then people, and last of all himself.** No doubt it is a narrow gate that a person denies himself, abnigates it in everything, forbearing the cuffs on the cheek and turning the other one also. If anyone compels him to go one mile, he goes with him two, and if anyone wants to sue him and take away his tunic, he lets him have his cloak also (Matt.5:39-41).

Enduring offences and forgiving those who abuse us may not be easy for many. More difficult still is the love for enemies and doing good to those who hate us (Matt.5:44). The spiritual person should forbear everything, relinquish everything, rise above the ordinary standard and hate himself for the sake of the Lord who said: *"...whoever loses his life for My sake will find it"* (Matt.16:25). It is not a light matter for the beginner in the spiritual path. He may feel agitated until he trains himself on perfect love. How truthful are the words of the Holy Bible: ***"We must through many***

tribulations enter the kingdom of God" (Acts 14:22)! He who walks in the path of God needs to ascend continually to the cross according to the Lord's words: *"...carry his cross and follow Me"* (Matt.16:24). To this effect Saint Paul the Apostle said: *"I have been crucified with Christ; it is no longer I who live, but Christ lives in me"* (Gal.2:20). **How profound is the term *"no longer I"!* No one can say it except he who entered by the narrow gate,** he who is trained always to hide himself so that the Lord may appear and so that others may be manifest. The phrase *"no longer I"* is also said by the humble person who insists in every circumstance to be last of all and the servant of all, always taking the last seat according to the Apostle's words: *"...in honour giving preference to one another"* (Rom.12:10). The phrase *"no longer I"* is said by the meek person who is lowly in heart who is utterly convinced from within that he is nothing.

Who can endure these things except the one who always enters by the narrow gate, not esteeming his own personal opinion in any matter and leaning not on his own understanding (Prov.3:5)? He prefers others to himself, placing himself below everyone. He does not resist nor is he wise in his own eyes (Rom.12:16). He censures himself in order that others may be justified. He carries others' sins that they may be innocent and he guilty. And in the depth of his love he redeems everyone as Christ the Lord did.

Toil for the Sake of God

Undoubtedly the narrow gate entails that a person toils for the Lord. He toils in carrying out the commandments which may appear too difficult to keep. He toils for the sake of giving comfort to others. Let us take Moses the Prophet as an example. It was easy for him to remain in Pharaoh's house as a prince enjoying honour, riches and rank. But he esteemed the reproach of Christ greater riches than all the treasures of Pharaoh. Not only that, but he chose *"rather to suffer affliction with the people of God than to enjoy the passing pleasures of sin"* (Heb.11:25). As a prophet and shepherd he laboured much in leading a stiff-necked people. He endured their rebellion and disobedience. He endured this for a long time with an open heart forbearing the faults of others.

All the prophets, all the pastors and all the ministers toiled for the sake of the Lord. We now venerate them, but in their generations they lived in bitter tribulations. Saint Athanasius the Apostolic, who defended the Faith strongly and with deep understanding, was an example of this. At times he was told: "The whole world is against you, Athanasius!"

Another example is Saint Paul the Apostle in comparison with the rest of the Apostles: *"in labours more abundant, in stripes above measure, in prisons more frequently, in deaths often... in weariness and toil, in sleeplessness often, in hunger and thirst, in fastings often, in cold and nakedness"* (2Cor.11:23-27). This Apostle said of himself and his fellow ministers in tribulations: *"But in all things we commend ourselves as ministers of God: in much patience, in tribulations, in needs, in distresses, in stripes, in imprisonments, in tumults, in labours, in sleeplessness, in fastings;... by honour and dishonour, by evil report and good report"* (2Cor.6:4-8), *"We are hard pressed on every side, yet not crushed; we are perplexed, but not in despair; persecuted, but not forsaken; struck down, but not destroyed- always carrying about in the body the dying of the Lord Jesus"* (2Cor.4:8-10).

The Narrow Gate Is For All

The principle of the narrow gate is for all, for every believer. Even the great Saint the Virgin Mary, the purest of all the people of the world, entered by the narrow gate. She lived an orphan and in poverty. She gave birth to her Son in a manger. She was estranged from her country, endured affliction, and saw her only Son, the Perfect and the Holy One, treated unjustly and crucified. In her, the words of Simeon the elder: *"...a sword will pierce through your own soul"* (Lk.2:35), were fulfilled.

Just as the Virgin Saint Mary went through tribulations so did John the Apostle, the most beloved Apostle of the Lord. He was imprisoned, scourged and exiled. Likewise were the rest of the Apostles. Also all the martyrs and confessors entered by the narrow gate. That is why the Church raises them higher than all the saints. In all their tortures and sufferings they proved the depth of their love for the Lord, so He rewarded them in the land of the living with ineffable ranks.

Assessing Tribulations

God never forgets any toil or tribulation which a believer endures for His sake. Even to the angel of the church of Ephesus who left his first love, He says: *"I know your works, your labour, your patience...and you have persevered and have patience, and have laboured for My name's sake and have not become weary"* (Rev.2:2,3). Inasmuch as man labours here on earth, so shall his reward be in the blissful eternity, according to the words of the Apostle: *"For our light affliction, which is but for a moment, is working for us a far more exceeding and eternal weight of glory"* (2Cor.4:17), and: *"the sufferings of this present time are not worthy to be compared with the glory which shall be revealed in us"* (Rom.8:18).

An important point which I would like to say about the narrow gate is that it is only narrow at the beginning. No sooner does the spiritual aspirant get used to it than he finds in it spiritual delight.

A Journey Towards Perfection

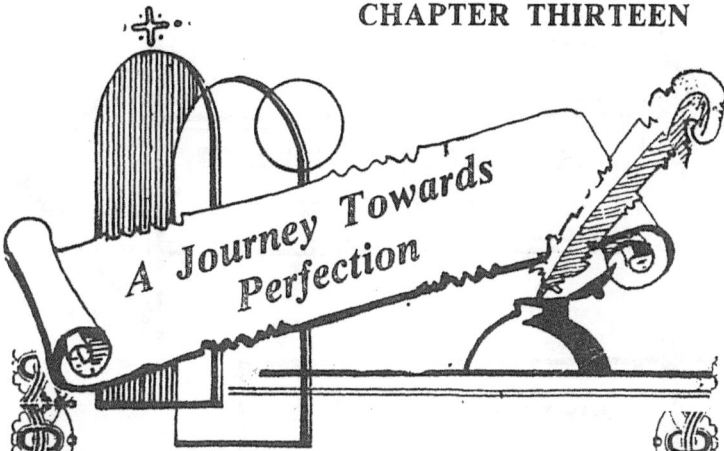

CHAPTER THIRTEEN

A Journey Towards Perfection

Growth and Perfection

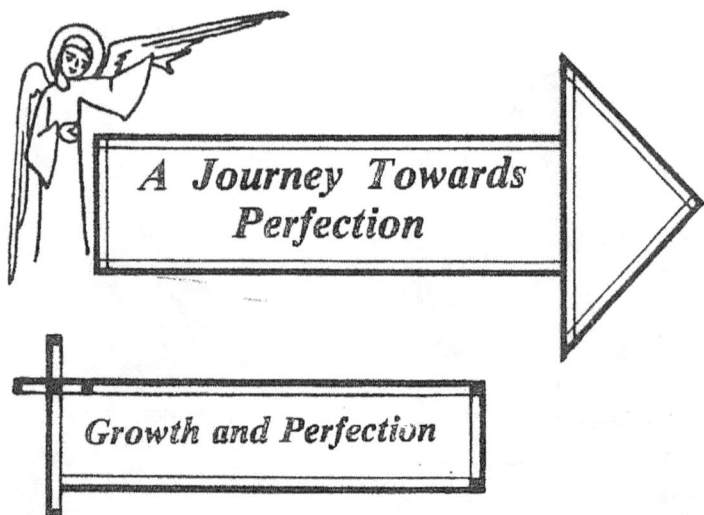

Some think that, having abandoned sin, they have attained to God and are walking in the spiritual path. **But abandoning sin represents only the passive struggle in the spiritual life. What about the positive side? This is a long journey.** That is why the spiritual life does not stop at all at a certain point. It is an unceasing walk, growing and advancing at all times. Thus the life of growth is one of the characteristics of the spiritual path.

To what does Christ the Lord liken spiritual growth? He likens the Kingdom of heaven to a man who should *"scatter seed on the ground, and should sleep by night and rise by day, and the seed should sprout and grow, he himself does not know how. For the earth yields crops by itself: first the blade, then the head, after that the full grain in the head"* (Mk.4:26-28).

Thus the spiritual man is likened to a tree which continually grows without ceasing for one second. The tree grows in a calm manner. Its growth may not be

259

noticed by you when you pass it everyday, but it does grow, and its growth is manifest after a while. It is written: *"The righteous shall flourish like a palm tree, he shall grow like a cedar in Lebanon"* (Ps.92:12). He grows in every element of the spiritual life. He grows in the knowledge of God and in the love of God. He grows in the life of purity and in prayer and contemplation.

Here we notice an important point, that he who does not grow is susceptible to listlessness or rather is liable to revert. This is similar to the car which as long as it is running, keeps its heat. However, if it stops, it loses its heat. Likewise is the continual walk in the spiritual life. It gives ardour to the heart which is the core of the person's relationship with God and with people. But to what extent does the spiritual man grow? He grows to holiness according to the words of Saint Peter the Apostle: *"...but as He who called you is holy, you also be holy in all your conduct"* (1Pet.1:15).

Therefore, it is an extensive call for holiness and this is the standard which the Lord requests from us. In this respect Saint Paul the Apostle says: *"...just as He chose us in Him before the foundation of the world, that we should be holy and without blame before Him in love"* (Eph.1:4).

The question then is not mere repentance but it is the life of holiness which befits the believers. But rather, the word 'saint' was the title of every faithful during the Apostolic Era. Saint Paul the Apostle says at the conclusion of his Epistle to the Philippians which he wrote from Rome: *"Greet every saint in Christ Jesus. The brethren who are with me greet you. All the saints greet you, but especially those who are of Caesar's household"* (Phil.4:21,22).

Do you live in this holiness, having become a member of all the saints? Or do you still rise and fall, fluctuating between life with God and life with the world? Holiness is not designed for the few spiritual elite, but it is the aim of everyone: *"perfecting holiness in the fear of God"* (2Cor.7:1), because *"this is the will of God, your sanctification"* (1Thess.4:3). In the Lord's Sermon on the Mount He made the beholding of God in eternity conditioned upon purity, saying: **"Blessed are the pure in heart, for they shall see God"** (Matt.5:8). Have you then reached the purity and holiness without which no one can see the Lord?

We also say that holiness alone is not sufficient but there must be growth in holiness so that the spiritual person may attain perfection. Of course perfection here is meant to be a relative perfection because absolute perfection is an attribute of God alone. The relative perfection is the perfection to which man can reach within his capabilities, and according to the extent of grace God endows upon him and the circumstances that surround him. Regarding this perfection the Lord said: **"Therefore you shall be perfect, just as your Father in heaven is perfect"** (Matt.5:48).

Therefore in your spiritual life you have to grow in purity and in holiness in order to reach perfection, the perfection of your capabilities and the perfection of your conduct, until you return to the Divine image after which you were created (Gen.1:27).

Who can attain this perfection? If you cannot, whatever you do and no matter how much you strive in the life of the Spirit, stand before God as a sinner and a delinquent because you are requested to be perfect whilst you are remote from it. That is why when the saints said about themselves that they were sinners, it was not a type of exaggeration or humbleness on their part, but it was because they felt their inadequacy before the perfection requested of them.

Since perfection is unlimited, therefore spiritual growth is likewise unlimited. I liken the man who pursues perfection to the person who pursues the horizon. He stands and sees the horizon from afar and it appears where heaven seems to touch the earth. So he goes there and finds that the horizon is over the sea. He goes to the sea and crosses it but he finds the horizon to be over the mountain, and so on forever. If such is the case, then meditate on the words of the Lord in His Gospel: *"...when you have done all those things which you are commanded, say, 'We are unprofitable servants'"* (Lk.17:10). And the Lord gave us many commandments which we have not yet carried out. And even if we have carried out all the commandments it is our duty to say that we are unprofitable servants because we have only done the things we are commanded to do and did not go beyond them towards perfection.

Believe me, the stage of *unprofitable servants* is a high level which we have not yet attained. No doubt the path is long before us and we have not walked in it yet, and need with all humility of heart to start.

There is another verse in the Holy Bible before which I stand at a loss. This verse is said by Saint Paul the Apostle in his Epistle to the Ephesians: *"...that you, being rooted and grounded in love, may be able to comprehend with all the saints what is the width and length and depth and height- to know the love of Christ which passes knowledge; that you may be filled with all the fullness of God"* (Eph.3:17-19).

God knows, I still stand bewildered before this verse. I have not reached any of its marvellous depths. I will try to refer to the meditations of the Fathers on this verse that I may know. If I reach anything I will inform you because here the Spirit works and not the mind or the intellect. Who can reach this fullness? It is requested from us all as ordered by the Apostle in the same epistle: *"...be filled with the Spirit"* (Eph.5:18). The Apostle said elsewhere: *"Walk in the Spirit"* (Gal.5:16), and called us to acquire the fruit of the Spirit (Gal.5:22).

Therefore, the path is long before us and needs great seriousness to walk along it. The spiritual person needs to pass the stage of repentance, reach the stages of purity and holiness, and then enter into the height and depth and the knowledge of Christ. Then he should pass from walking in the Spirit to all the fruits of the Spirit, to the Spirit-filled life and to perfection.

That is why we see Saint Paul the Apostle saying: *"Not that I have already attained, or am already perfected; but I press on, that I may lay hold of that for which Christ Jesus has also laid hold of me"* (Phil.3:12). Saint Paul, who was caught up into the third heaven, to Paradise (2Cor.12:4), who laboured more than the twelve Apostles in travelling and preaching, who wrote fourteen epistles, who was thrown into prison and tortured for the sake of the Lord, who performed many miracles and had numerous revelations, and who spoke in tongues more than all others, says finally: *"I do not count myself to have apprehended; but one thing I do"*. We ask him: What is it?

He replies: *"...forgetting those things which are behind and reaching forward to those things which are ahead"* (Phil.3:13). He forgets all those great gifts, all his labour in the ministry, forgets that he was caught up into the third heaven, and presses on toward the goal. He presses on that he may apprehend. Apprehend what? Apprehend the *"upward call of God in Christ Jesus"* (Phil.3:14); apprehend this wonderful fullness.

That is why he exhorts us saying: *"Run in such a way that you may obtain it"* (1Cor.9:24), and says with us: *"Therefore I run thus"* (1Cor.9:26), and he also says: *"Therefore, let us as many as are mature, have this mind"* (Phil.3:15). Therefore not only is it a call for beginners but also for the spiritually mature. A call for all to pursue the goal in order to apprehend.

There is another level placed before us as children of God, and all of us are called children of God. Saint John the Apostle says: *"Whoever has been born of God does not sin,* for His seed remains in him; and he cannot sin, because he has been born of God"* (1Jn.3:9) and: *"We know that whoever is born of God does not sin; but he who has been born of God keeps himself, and the wicked one does not touch him"* (1Jn.5:18).

Have you reached this level in which you cannot sin and the wicked one does not touch you? Here is a unique standard! It is not resisting sin, nor is it striving against sin and overcoming it but it is the standard of a saintly person who cannot sin. Who has reached such perfection? Nevertheless, I do not want to present you with the standards of the New Testament which entail sublimation but I will take you to a commandment of the Old Testament, which is, *"You shall love the Lord your God with all your heart, with all your soul, and with all your might"* (Deut.6:5). Who has reached the love of God with all his heart? The word *'all'* means that nothing exists in the heart other than God. There is no other love in the heart competing with the love for God.

Undoubtedly, this means complete mortification to the world. It means detachment and filling the heart with the love of God. Have you made a start on this path? **Have you started with the fear of God which is the first step that leads to love** according to the words of the Holy Bible: *"The fear of the Lord is the beginning of wisdom"* (Prov.9:10)? The fear of God means obeying Him and submitting to His commandments. Thus you reach the love of God and enter into His kingdom. To this effect the Holy Bible says: *"The kingdom of God is within you"*. Do you feel that the Kingdom is within you? Have you begun to foretaste the Kingdom? Have you received the pledge in your present life that you will enjoy the Kingdom fully in the next world?

Start then by foretasting the Kingdom. When you pray and say, *"Your kingdom come"*, pray that His kingdom come into your heart and your mind, your senses and your body and your feelings. Then you will sing, saying, *"The Lord reigns"* (Ps.97:1). **But you may ask after all these: "What shall I do when the path is long before me?"** The matter should not be dealt with by despair or sadness, nor by saying: "There is no use of me". All these are stratagem of the devil, through which he tries to make you fall into pusillanimity that you may despondently cease your striving, or feel that the life with God is heavy. The best advice to give you is that the **beginning of the longest journey is a single step. Therefore start with this one step** no matter how short or weak or lukewarm it is. Then when God sees your desire to live with Him He will send you Divine support and His grace will visit you and His Holy Spirit will work strongly in you.

God who worked in the saints and helped them to attain perfection is capable of working in you. However, the grace of God is not an encouragement for your slackness, negligence and carelessness but it works with you. Thus you enter into communion with God, to work for the sake of His kingdom; His kingdom within you and within others.

God is capable of uplifting you in one step as He did with some of the saints of repentance such as Saint Augustine whom He transformed from the depth of sin to the depth of theologies, contemplating the Divine attributes, and to the depth of His love. This He also did with Saint Mary of Egypt whom He took from foulness to the monastic life and hermitage, and she became one of the great saints.

If God desires for you gradualness in the life of the Spirit, may His will be done. This is what He did with Saint Moses the Black whom He lead gradually towards repentance, gradually endowing him with the spiritual virtues, eradicating from him obduracy and granting him love for all people, wonderful meekness and humility of heart, and he became a different man.

The important thing, then, is to offer your heart to God that He may fill it with His love. Say to Him: "Lord, I am unable to attain to Your love because there are secular, materialistic and bodily love attracting me, and I am weak before them. Therefore, I want You to grant me Your love as a free endowment and gift from You, as the Apostle said: '...because the love of God has been poured out in our hearts by the Holy Spirit who was given to us'" (Rom.5:5). At the same time in which you ask God to work with you, you also work with Him. Work with all your potentialities. Do not slacken at all in your spirituality. Be serious. Open your heart that God may fill it. Be circumspect not to open it for any erroneous love. **Keep away diligently from everything that separates you from God. The little which you offer God will be accepted by Him and will be very precious in His sight, as He accepted the two mites of the widow.**

God knows the extent of your potentialities and does not request from you more than them. But He will rather bless the few things which you have so that they may become many and grant you greater insight. In this way He leads you gradually by His grace to where He wills for you. Therefore, do not look at the end of the path and despair, but look only at this first single step and ensure that you walk it well. The more faithful you are in the few things, the more God will commend to you, according to His truthful promise.

Hindrances to Growth

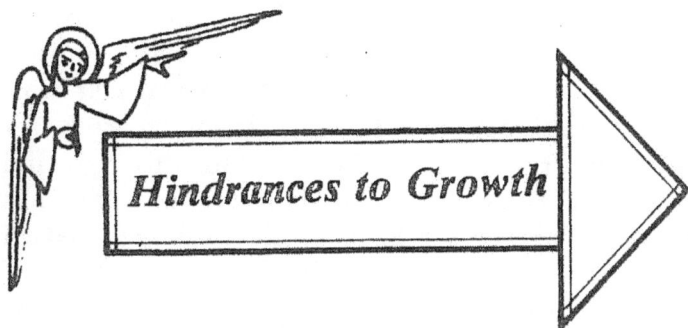

We have talked about growth and its necessity in the spiritual life, and how it is an outstanding characteristic of the sound conduct along the spiritual path. We also said that spiritual growth is a stage towards perfection. Now we ask: **Does every person grow in his spirituality? And does every spiritual growth continue?** It is obvious that the growth of many is sometimes impeded. They halt at a certain stage in their spiritual life, or rather even revert at times. What are the reasons for this? What are the hindrances that impede spiritual growth?

Hindrances vary from one person to another. However we will try to speak here about a few of the general hindrances that deter growth.

1. The Devils' Combats

Satan does not rest when he finds a person continually advancing in his spiritual path. He must rise against him. **This is sometimes called 'the envy of the devils'.** They envy those who advance in their love for God because they lost this beautiful union with God and lost His kingdom. That is why they fight not just the spiritual growth but the whole spiritual path. For this reason the Book of Sirach says: *"My son, if you come forward to serve the Lord, prepare yourself for temptation"* (Sir.2:1). The Church reads this verse and the whole chapter on the occasion of ordaining monks because he who enters the monastic life tries to make a start on the life of perfection. The Church also reads this chapter in the prayer of the Third Hour of Tuesday of the Holy Pascha because on that day the Lord Jesus Christ approached to accomplish the work of the great Redemption and enter into His array of trials. **That is why quite often no sooner does a spiritual person walk in the path of growth than he finds the world upturned against him.** Some struggle against these spiritual wars diligently with all their efforts and with all the work of grace within them. They prevail and continue to grow, whereas others collapse and weaken, and are unable to advance in their growth.

When Satan found the work of Redemption was about to be accomplished he waged his severe wars against the Apostles. The Lord Jesus Christ said to them: *"Indeed, Satan has asked for you, that he may sift you as wheat"* (Lk.22:31). Through this sifting the spiritual growth of the Apostles halted and some of them retreated. Many of the saints and prophets passed through such sifting because Satan does not leave anyone without combat.

If you encounter such warfare do not be troubled. It is natural. It is part of the nature of the spiritual path and it is part of the nature of the devils. Nonetheless, struggle as best you can. And in every fresh step you ascend up the spiritual ladder expect an attack to stop your growth, and be prepared. **If you find a combat in every new spiritual endeavour you walk in for your spiritual growth, rest assured.** Unless Satan feared such practice he would not have resisted you and waged his war against you. It is a healthy sign on your part and an ill sign on Satan's part. However, wars are one thing and lapses are another. The history of the monk and hermit fathers is full of spiritual combats waged against them for the purpose of halting their growth. **Combats are simply attempts from Satan. They may succeed at times and fail at others.** Satan is an enemy of spiritual growth. He has to fight growth at any cost whatever happens. However, he is not the only obstacle against spiritual growth. There are many of his allies of which we mention:

2. The Thwarting Environment

Bad environment impedes spiritual growth. **Therefore, in the spiritual path, select your friends, your companions and the people you associate with.** They may impede your growth, or even cause you to revert. In the same way that a good friend pulls you up with him, likewise a bad friend pulls you down and impedes your growth. The unspiritual husband hampers the spiritual growth of his wife, and vice versa. Together they share one life. The condition for companionship is compatibility. The absence of compatibility impedes spiritual growth and even, you may say, the whole life.

The spiritual growth of our father Abraham the Patriarch was impeded for a period of time because of the surrounding environment. He was hindered when he was estranged in Gerar. He knew that there was no fear of God in that place and feared that its people might kill him because of his wife (Gen.20:11). Fear prompted him to say that Sarah was his sister, and thus Abimelech took her. That environment, which was void of the fear of God, not only hampered the growth of the great patriarch but rather caused him to fall into lapses.

The same situation occurred with the righteous Lot but on a greater scale in the land of Sodom. Saint Peter the Apostle said of him: *"...for that righteous man, dwelling among them, tormented his righteous soul from day to day by seeing and hearing their lawless deeds"*, and *"was oppressed with the filthy conduct of the wicked"* (2Pet.2:8).

Therefore, bad environment and external oppressions can impede even prophets and righteous men. Because even if a righteous person prevails for a while, yet when the environment constrains him day after day, his righteous soul may suffer, causing his growth to cease.

For this reason, in your spiritual practices, be circumspect not to accompany anyone who may impede your growth. On the day when you partake of the Holy Communion or practise the Sacrament of Confession, being in an advanced spiritual state, be on your guard not to converse with a friend on a subject that might agitate the purity of your heart and mind.

Our Fathers benefitted from the solitary life. They lived in solitude away from the environment that would preoccupy them or hamper their growth. They devoted themselves to their spiritual work with God, away from the obstacles of the environment. In the same manner lived all those who loved solitude even whilst they were in the world. They did not falter between two parties; they did not spend some time in spiritual ardour and others in causes that cooled down their fervour.

In the Parable of the Sower we hear about the thorns that choke the plants after their growth (Matt.13), so be circumspect and keep away from the thorns so that your holy cultivation may grow without being choked by the surrounding environment. And in your growth remember the words of the poet:
When will the edifice be complete
If you construct and another deletes?

3. Self-satisfaction in Spirituality

This is when a person reaches a certain spiritual level without advancing any further, not considering passing beyond that level, thinking that it is the end. **Or it is when a person is attacked by the devil who says to him that beyond that level is a type of excessiveness.** But our saintly Fathers were never satisfied with their spiritual attainment, but continually struggled to attain to a better state. Saint Paul the Apostle was caught up into the third heaven, yet he said: *"One thing I do, forgetting those things which are behind and reaching forward to those things which are ahead"* (Phil.3:13).

He whose growth ceases is prone to deteriorate.

Therefore try always to grow. Never be satisfied with your present condition but wisely place before you the high levels of attainment of the Fathers so that you may be encouraged to increase your striving. Know an important principle, that is: **There is a great difference between growth and excessiveness.** Wisdom is your scale of discrimination. However, Satan may use one of the two expressions in place of the other to fight you.

4. The Wrong Counsel

Wrong counsel hampers the spiritual growth if the spiritual advisor is not experienced in spiritual matters or if he has personal motives. For example, there are advisors who lead their disciples to carry out the commandments literally after the manner of the scribes and the Pharisees. And the Lord Jesus Christ said: *"And if the blind leads the blind, both will fall into a ditch"* (Matt.15:14).

Therefore, joyful is he who is under a wise, experienced and discreet guide. However, the person has to scrutinize everything and cling only to the best (1Thess.5:21). Also do not follow just anyone's advice nor seek the guidance of anyone, as is said: **"Receive education from the educated and seek wisdom from the wise".**

5. The Wrong Emulation

We mean when a person clothes himself with another personality without discernment, or employs literally what is recorded in the 'Lives of the Desert Fathers' or in the life stories of the saints without knowing what suits him personally, and without knowing the intermediate levels in which that particular saint walked until he reached the level recorded in his life story.

Emulation can be of what is recorded in books or of contemporary persons or of the father confessor. Each of these personalities, however, possesses a different nature and the style which suits them psychologically and spiritually may not suit the person who emulates them.

The father confessor himself may be the one who encourages such emulation when he wants his disciples to be copies of him however different their natures may be. And as a result of walking in a path incompatible to his nature, the person's spiritual growth is hindered. For example, a father confessor likes social life and mixing with people whereas his spiritual son prefers tranquillity and stillness. If he compels his son to walk in the life of associating with people, his spiritual growth will cease.

6. Pride

Man may grow well in the spiritual path until he reaches a certain level. Then he starts to compare himself with those who are less than him. So his heart is puffed up. Then grace withdraws from him because of his pride. As a result he either lapses or his growth halts.

The gifts of the Lord are granted only to the humble who are uplifted through them. The humble person, no matter how high he is raised in his spiritual life, considers himself nothing, comparing himself with the high levels of the saints. That is why he calls himself a sinner. The Lord beholds his humility and endows him with further growth.

The person who grows and gets self-elated may become satisfied with his level. He does not strive to receive more, and so his growth ceases. **We fear haughtiness not only because of a halt in growth but also for fear of falling into lapses.** In this respect the Holy Bible says: *"Pride goes before destruction, and a haughty spirit before a fall"* (Prov. 16:18). If you are walking in the spiritual path be on your guard against self-elation lest you fall.

An example of the effect of pride on the cessation of growth is when a man is lifted up through the dispensation of grace and refers his uplifting to his personal efforts and self-righteousness and not to the work of God in him. **As a result grace withdraws from him because he attributed the support of grace which he received to himself.** As soon as grace leaves him he is unable to advance one step forward and may deteriorate.

7. The Disposition of Grace

The grace of God may withdraw from a person not because of his pride but for fear of him becoming proud. When grace withdraws from him he weakens and may fall into many errors so that these errors serve as a cause for his contrition in future. Probably this is what happened with Elijah the great prophet when he feared Jezebel (1Kin.19:14). And he was the one who did not fear King Ahab nor all the prophets of Baal and the concubines but greatly triumphed over them all on Mount Carmel (1Kin.18).

Probably a similar thing happened to David the great prophet on whom the Spirit of God descended. He lived the life of prayer and psalmody, after which he lapsed into some sins of beginners! This helped him afterwards in the life of contrition and tears.

8. Diversion Towards Administrative Matters

When a person leaves the spiritual work and turns to administrative matters, the administrative problems preoccupy him from his and others' salvation, causing him to slip into many errors hampering his growth. For example, a monk who lives in solitude on the mountain and grows in his spirituality is taken and put in charge of a position. The administrative matters are not sin in themselves but they preoccupy him from his spiritual work and cause his growth to cease. For this reason our saintly Fathers used to escape positions in order to devote their time to God. **This also happens when a priest who is successful in his spiritual work is put in charge of administrative matters in church. They hinder his spirituality and impede his growth.** Therefore if any of you is engaged in administrative matters let him examine himself whether he continues to grow or has halted or has deteriorated from his level.

9. Caring For the Outward Semblance of Virtue

This is when a person is concerned with the quantitative and not with the spiritual growth of his spiritual practices. He concerns himself with the number of psalms and not with the spirituality of praying them. He concerns himself with the number of prostrations and not with the spiritual way of making them, with the outward semblance of fasting, the period of abstinence and the quality and quantity of food and not with submitting the body and giving a chance to the spirit. In this manner he concerns himself with the outward semblances and not with the depth of the virtue, so his growth ceases. He cares to attain much prayer and not depth in prayer, much reading and not depth in reading nor contemplation of what he reads. As for you, concern yourself with the spirit, inner growth and the hidden virtues.

10. Misinterpretation

As Saint Abba Antony the Great said, the greatest of all virtues is discrimination which is the sound understanding of spiritual matters. Many people failed in their spirituality because they did not comprehend rightly the spiritual path and did not have a wise spiritual guide. They depended on their human efforts more than they did on God through prayer.

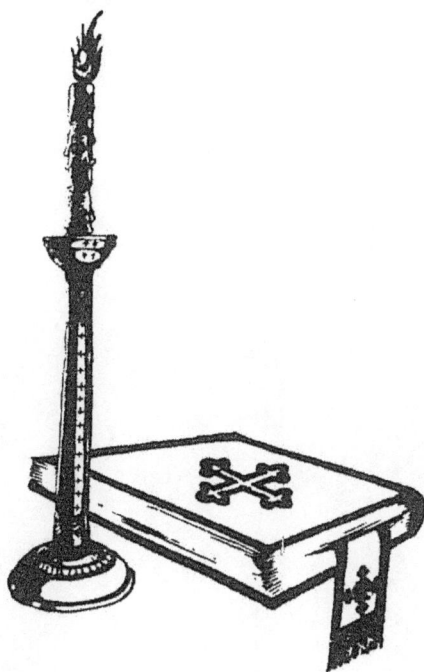